ARTIFICIAL INTELLIGENCE

WHY AI PROJECTS SUCCEED OR FAIL

KLAUS TRUEMPER

Softcover published by Leibniz Company
2304 Cliffside Drive
Plano, Texas, 75023
USA

Original edition March 2023
Updated editions May 2023, April 2024

The book is typeset in LATEX using the Tufte-style book class, which was inspired by the work of Edward R. Tufte and Richard Feynman.

Sources and licenses for all figures are listed in the Notes section.

Library of Congress Cataloging-in-Publication Data
Truemper, Klaus, 1942–

Artificial Intelligence: Why AI Projects Succeed or Fail
ISBN 978-0-9991402-5-3
1. Brain. 2. Neuroscience. 3. Wittgenstein.

Contents

1

Introduction

Artificial Intelligence (AI) is a strange area of science: Some projects succeed beyond all expectations, while others fail miserably. How is this possible? More importantly, how can one avoid failure? This book answers both questions.

Here are some examples of amazing AI successes of the last thirty years:

- The astonishing victory of the Deep Blue computer over the world's chess champion in 1997[1]
- The seemingly miraculous performance of the Google search engine invented in 1998[2]
- The amazing results achieved by neural machine translation systems such as DeepL and Google Translate, which have been able to translate both text and speech of multiple languages since the mid-2010s[3]
- The impressive way ChatGPT of 2022 summarizes complex information, draws conclusions from data, and even creates poems[4]

And here are examples of recent, major failures:

- IBM's much touted Watson Health expert system for medical diagnosis and treatment, which was based on the successful IBM

Watson software, produced so many wrong decisions that IBM shut it down.[5]

- During recent years, some heavily promoted self-driving cars have created mayhem, even produced death, when unleashed on urban traffic.[6]

- Neural nets—a frequently used tool for data interpretation in AI systems—often fail to produce reliable predictions. This aspect is called *fragility*.[7] The problems of self-driving cars can partly be traced to that shortcoming. Some instances of fragility:[8]

  - Misreading a stop sign due to a minor variation of the sign
  - Claiming that pictures displaying some abstract pattern depict an animal
  - Drastically changing the interpretation when a picture has been modified by a minute amount
  - Changing the interpretation abruptly when the displayed item is rotated

- Other failures of neural nets resulted from inappropriate selection of training data. For example, such data introduced a bias against women in an automated applicant evaluation system at Amazon.[9]

Causes of Failure

What sets the successes and failures apart? How can one generally avoid failures in the future?

Some failures are caused by erroneous mathematics or use of inappropriate data. The fragility of neural nets and the biased Amazon application software are instances.

But others defy such simple explanation. For example, the failure of Watson Health and the mayhem and death produced by certain self-driving cars isn't just due to some mathematical oversight or use of wrong data.

This book uses modern brain science and philosophy to obtain answers for the nonobvious cases. You may wonder: How is it possible that results of these two areas can explain such diverse successes and failures and also suggest corrective actions?

For the answer, let's pretend somebody has requested that we solve an AI problem. For example, we are to teach a computer how to drive a car in urban traffic, or are to design a computer program that translates text from one language to another one.

How would we proceed? Here are two useful steps. The first one seems rather simple and obvious, while the second one may appear abstract and convoluted. Please bear with us; we will justify the second step in a moment.

- By watching ourselves solve the problem—for example, how we drive a car—we infer how a computer can produce the same result.

- By thinking about the world, we infer how the world is structured. We assume that this insight into the structure of the world is correct and hence postulate that, when a computer looks at the world the same way, it will function like us.

We define "watching ourselves how we solve the problem" cited in the first step to be *mind observation* or *action observation*. Specifically, *mind observation* takes place when we observe our decision making, and *action observation* occurs when we track our actions.

We call the "insight into the structure of the world" mentioned in the second step the *web of facts* of the world. We then define the *web claim* to be the proposition that the web of facts indeed describes the world.

Mind and action observation and the web claim seem appropriate tools for AI projects, don't they? Indeed, in the first step we discover what the computer should do; in the second one, how the computer should consider the world at large. Yet, we see soon that both steps are not just inappropriate, but *virtually guarantee failure*.

The four successful AI systems cited above—the Deep Blue computer, the Google search engine, DeepL and Google Translate, and ChatGPT—supply supporting evidence. None of them depends on mind or action observation or the web claim.

On the other hand, the failure of the Watson Health expert system can be traced back to a system construction based on mind observation.

The mayhem and death produced by certain self-driving cars are mainly due to a system design based on action observation.

The web claim has played an important role in failures of natural language processing (NLP). For example, over decades it misguided the construction of translation methods.

The web claim even resulted in wrong philosophical results. For example, a major result of AI—the Chinese Room created in 1980 and debated since then—is wrong since it implicitly relies on the web claim.

How can we avoid mind and action observation and the erroneous web claim? It isn't easy since we carry within us an almost hypnotic belief in their correctness. But we can overcome that urge, as the cited successes demonstrate.

Let's look at the two main tools of our investigation.

Brain Science

Modern brain science started just 30 years ago. The numerous new results are like isolated pieces of a vast mosaic that, we hope, will eventually supply coherent insight into human reasoning.

The existing pieces are too disparate to be used by themselves for an investigation of the successes and failures of AI systems, let alone for proposals how failures could be avoided.

We have used those pieces to construct a hypothesis about their interaction that is consistent with all prior results and may be viewed as a rough approximation of human reasoning. We call it the *neuroprocess hypothesis*.

It is detailed enough that we can apply it in a variety of settings, yet simple enough that we can manipulate it and derive comprehensive conclusions. We employed it in the predecessor book *Wittgenstein and Brain Science*[10] to solve philosophical problems that had been open for centuries.

Roughly speaking, the hypothesis postulates that human decision making relies on conscious and subconscious neuroprocesses that interact in certain ways. By definition, we are not aware of the subconscious portion.

The lack of understanding of the subconscious portion is the root cause of the failure of mind or action observation. We watch ourselves thinking or acting and believe that we understand what a computer should do to replicate the results. Actually, the insight includes nothing about the performance of the complex subconscious neuroprocesses and hence is inadequate.

Brain science is technically known as *neuroscience*. We employ the latter term from now on to be consistent with the literature. Further motivation comes from the fact that the results used here involve not just the brain but the entire nervous system.

Let's turn to the second tool.

Philosophy

The philosopher Ludwig Wittgenstein (1889–1951) investigated how language expresses what's happening in the world. In particular, his book *Tractatus Logico-Philosophicus*, published in 1921 and usually referred to as the *Tractatus*, completely characterizes when a statement about the world is meaningful.

In the late 1920s, Wittgenstein realized that the main conclusion of the *Tractatus* is wrong and embarked on a very different approach to clarify the meaning and use of language.

The web claim is a simplified version of the complex results of the *Tractatus* and thus is wrong, as stated earlier.

Prior and Concurrent Work

Results dealing with intuitive or impulsive decisions are somewhat related. Excellent contributions are *Thinking, Fast and Slow* by D. Kahneman[11] and *The Invisible Gorilla: How Our Intuitions Deceive Us* by C. Chabris and D. Simons.[12]

In 2010, K. Friston defined the *free energy principle*.[13] It says that all living systems aim to minimize surprise when they interact with the world, in the following sense: They anticipate what will happen, and use any deviation from the forecast to modify the environment or adapt to the change.

Based on that principle, Friston started a broad research program in AI. The work involves a number of collaborators. The extensive effort has begun to shed light on the neuroprocesses and their interaction with each other, the rest of the body, and the world.

In some sense, the research develops AI theory from the ground up, starting with the free energy principle. The main tool of the construction is mathematics. The sciences, in particular neuroscience, supply the data.

The free energy principle and the earlier mentioned neuroprocess hypothesis are connected. As shown in Chapter 5, the hypothesis postulates that the neuroprocesses build, update, and use *models* to accomplish their interaction with each other, the body, and the world. This is a macro view of the neuroprocesses. The free energy principle is the fundamental explanation why and how these models are created, revised, and employed.

A detailed survey article lays out the depth and breath of the prior/concurrent research. It ends with the following statement:[14]

"[W]e need to explore computational models for world model learning and inference to build both a human-like intelligence and to understand the human brain. By developing models and algorithms and by testing through biological, computational, and robotic experiments, we aspire to a better understanding of the two sides of the same coin; namely, intelligence."

―――――――――

The chapters of the next part describe the neuroprocess hypothesis in detail. The material is taken from the predecessor book *Wittgenstein and Brain Science*.[15] If you have read that book, you may skip ahead to Chapter 7 and start on the discussion of AI.

Part I

Neuroprocess
Hypothesis

2

Interaction with the World

This chapter and Chapter 3 lay the groundwork for the discussion of the neuroprocess hypothesis. Here we look at the way we interact with the world. The key components of that interaction are *models*. What are they? There is no simple answer since the model concept is so widely used. Here are some examples.

- *Models* who display dresses in a fashion show
- *Car models* of a particular design
- *Model species* that are mimicked by another species
- *Scale models* of airplanes in a wind tunnel
- *Weather models* forecasting the movement of hurricanes
- *Economic models* anticipating a recession

The last three are *models of the world*. In this chapter we examine the role of such models in our lives.

Models of the World

In the night sky some bright points of light seem to always move together, while others wander individually. Extensive research carried out over centuries eventually resulted in a mathematical model that not only classifies the two types of lights as stars and planets, but predicts their movement with reasonable precision. The astronomer and mathematician Johannes Kepler (1571–1630) accomplished this feat in 1627.[16] In particular, his model predicts that the planets move around the sun in elliptical orbits.

The results of the model are often cited as if they were facts of the world: The orbits of the planets around the sun are then claimed *to be* elliptical.

But that is not the case: The planets influence each other in ways that have proved to be mathematically intractable: While approximate formulas predict the movement for limited time intervals, we can only guess what will happen long-term.[17]

Models and Facts

The example isn't an unusual case of model interpretation. We generally conflate model output with facts of the world. We do this, for example, when models explain

- the bond forces within molecules
- the flow of electricity
- the strength of materials
- the conversion of heat into power in engines
- the vibrations of strings of a violin
- the echo in a valley
- the Great Depression

The conflation has provided us with deep insight into the world. Using that knowledge we have created equipment with miraculous performance: airplanes, computers, satellites, spacecraft, the global positioning system, artificial hearts, ... The list is endless.

Appropriately, the theoretical physicist and cosmologist S. Hawking called this conflation *model-dependent realism*.[18]

The conflation is aided by our experience that many of our sense perceptions—but by no means all—are shared by others.[19] Accordingly, these perceptions are in some sense impersonal, and we develop the feeling that they are facts of the world. That pragmatic view simplifies the interaction with others.

But the conclusion that our perceptions are facts is unjustified. If a number of people agree with us on a sense perception, it only means that they have adopted similar or identical models.

———————

Until recently, the construction of models didn't extend to the nervous system since suitable investigative tools didn't exist. That has changed. For example, functional magnetic resonance imaging (fMRI) allows us to observe the brain in action. These tools have produced a flood of diverse results.

The next chapter describes some of the new insights.

3

Results of Neuroscience

The human *nervous system* consists of the *brain*, the *spinal cord*, and the *network of nerves* that connect the brain and the spinal cord to other parts of the human body, for example, to the eyes, ears, organs, muscles, blood vessels, and glands.[20]

Structure

Neuroscientists have established a rich theory about the structure and performance of the nervous system. Here are some results about the brain.[21]

- The traditional view that each region of the brain is dedicated to a particular function has been replaced by the insight that neuroprocesses allocate regions dynamically, for example, for handling hearing, sight, smell, taste, and touch. Hence there is no visual brain, or auditory brain, or sense-of-touch brain.

- The neuroprocesses for the various functions compete with each other for space in the brain since there is only a finite amount of real estate, so to speak.

- Hours, days, weeks, and years after birth, neuroprocesses learn to interpret incoming signals and produce appropriate output.

For example, they learn so that the person can grab items, interpret images, understand speech, walk, and talk.

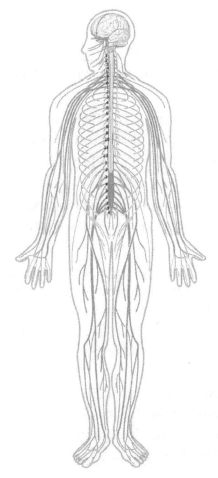

Nervous system diagram.[22]

Plasticity

Neuroprocesses can overcome the effects of catastrophic damage to the brain.[23]

- The neuroprocesses cope with misfortune—such as a person going blind, losing hearing, or losing a limb—by reallocating no-longer-needed capacity to existing functions.

- In exceptional cases, the neuroprocesses can reconfigure the brain even when half of the brain was removed at a very young age to combat an incurable disease.

  A similar adjustment takes place when half of the brain is missing at birth.

- In cases of severe hearing loss, a cochlear implant captures sound and sends it electrically, through the cochlea, to the auditory nerve.[24] The neuroprocesses adapt to the new format of audio signals.

- For a deaf person, sound is sometimes converted externally to touch—that is, auditory signals become pressure signals on the skin. After a while, the person "hears" via the skin.

- For a blind person, images are sometimes converted to pressure on the skin. After some training, the person "sees" via the skin. When images are converted to electrotactile shocks on the tongue, the person eventually "sees" via the tongue. When images are converted to sound, a person begins to "see" via earbuds.

  This may sound crazy, but is not. For the case of "seeing" with the tongue, brain imaging has shown that the signals received by the tongue are processed in an area of the brain that normally handles visual motion.

Enteric Nervous System

Parts of the nervous system outside the brain independently carry out processes at a very sophisticated level. An example is the *enteric nervous system (ENS)*. It is embedded in the lining of the gastrointestinal tract from the esophagus to the rectum. Its operation is so sophisticated that it has been nicknamed the *second brain*.[25] It is in constant communication with the brain. For example, it alerts the brain when more food is needed or, conversely, when food intake should stop.

––––––––––––––––––––

So far we have provided an intuitive understanding of the neuro-processes. The next chapter supplies details.

4

Fatigue

We are hiking in the mountains: We climb up slopes and descend into valleys, all the time enjoying the scenery. After four hours, we feel tired and decide to rest.[26]

Where does this feeling come from?

First Explanation

An obvious explanation is: The leg muscles determine that they have been stressed and are tired. They send corresponding information to the brain, which translates it to a feeling of fatigue.

Suppose that vague explanation is correct, and a person's statement such as "My legs are getting tired" captures the essence of the situation.

How then is the following possible?

In 1986, Georges Holtyzer of Belgium walked 418 miles in six and a half days. He was not permitted any stops for rest and moved almost 99 percent of the time.[27]

Why do we get a feeling of fatigue after four hours of hiking when Holtyzer could walk more than six days without rest?

Second Explanation

Research into the causes of fatigue started in the 19th century. It led to the explanation that lack of oxygen and build-up of lactate caused muscle fatigue.

Exercise textbooks from the 1930s to today advance this theory.[28] Here are some problems with that claim:[29]

- Even at peak exertion, only about two-thirds of available muscle fibers are active.
- The feeling of fatigue is delayed when music is played during the activity—as is invariably done at exercise clubs around the world.
- When a wall clock is slowed down, people become tired later.

So, something else must be happening.

Emotion

The crucial insight came during the 2010s, when fatigue was recognized as an emotion:[30] The feeling of fatigue is produced by a subconscious neuroprocess to ensure that ongoing physical efforts don't overtax the body.

This insight supports the following explanation of fatigue:

- A subconscious neuroprocess analyzes the performance of the physical body and decides whether the current effort if continued not just for hours but days would cause damage. We aren't consciously aware of this analysis.
- Once the subconscious neuroprocess arrives at that conclusion, it outputs a feeling of fatigue. We recognize that feeling and decide to rest. We can restate this as: A conscious neuroprocess becomes aware of the feeling and concludes that rest is needed.

Thus, fatigue is an emotion that protects the body from harm.

Subconscious Neuroprocesses

The fatigue example is a special case of the following general situation.

- A subconscious neuroprocess receives input from outside or inside the body. Visual and audio signals are input examples from outside the body, while heart rate and oxygen saturation of the blood are input from the inside.

- The subconscious neuroprocess takes the input and produces various conclusions for conscious neuroprocesses. Example outputs are *feelings*, *images*, *interpreted audio*, and *interpreted writing*. The subconscious neuroprocess may also initiate *direct actions* that affect the body or the world.

The example list for the conclusions is woefully incomplete. In fact, we are unable to give a complete characterization of the possible cases. Instead, we simply declare all cases outside feelings and direct actions to be *unbidden thoughts*. The term "unbidden" reflects the fact that the thoughts pop up in consciousness and aren't the result of conscious reasoning.

For example, when a subconscious neuroprocess has analyzed a scene sensed by the eyes, we call the resulting image that pops into consciousness an unbidden thought.

Output to Consciousness

In summary, we consider just three types of output of subconscious neuroprocesses: feelings, unbidden thoughts, and direct actions. The feelings and unbidden thoughts are supplied to conscious neuroprocesses.

- *Feelings*: Examples are fatigue, fear, and joy.
- *Unbidden thoughts*: They suddenly pop up in consciousness. For example, a subconscious process initiates a panic attack by the

frightening thought "My heart has stopped." Another case is the image resulting from visual information, or the recognition of spoken words from audio.

- *Direct actions*: Examples range from control of the heartbeat and respiratory rate to the movement of the fingers when a piano virtuoso plays a demanding concerto. In the latter case, the time available for triggering the movement of the fingers is far too short for conscious control.

The conscious neuroprocesses manipulate the feelings and unbidden thoughts supplied by the subconscious neuroprocesses using *deliberate thoughts*, and finally produce *decisions* and *actions*. We use the term "deliberate" for the thoughts since we can justify them by a logical argument or other explanation.

Direct Action

The direct actions of the subconscious neuroprocesses aren't part of the input for the conscious neuroprocesses. However, another subconscious neuroprocess may observe such an action and output its occurrence as an unbidden thought to consciousness. We say "may" since that step need not take place. For example, conscious neuroprocesses usually do not become aware of changes of the heart rate, while the knee jerk triggered by a tap below the knee is felt and seen.

You may wonder: The above definitions seemingly preclude that two subconscious neuroprocesses send information to each other. If we come upon two neuroprocesses with that feature, we eliminate the case conceptually by considering the two neuroprocesses to be just one neuroprocess. In some sense, we merge the two neuroprocesses.

Assumption About Neuroprocesses

We emphasize that the subconscious and conscious neuroprocesses are models of the actual processes in the human body. The discussion of Chapter 2 fully applies to these models. In particular, we invoke the idea of model-dependent realism and conflate model results with facts about the human body.

We may restate this as follows.

> *From now on, we act as if the subconscious and conscious neuroprocesses take place in the human body.*

Summary

We have defined the following inputs and outputs of the neuroprocesses:[31]

- Subconscious neuroprocess
  - input: information of body and world
  - output: feelings and unbidden thoughts for conscious neuroprocesses, and direct actions
- Conscious neuroprocess
  - input: feelings and unbidden thoughts from subconscious neuroprocesses
  - output: decisions and actions established via deliberate thoughts

----

We emphasize that the subconscious neuroprocesses are connected with the conscious ones beyond the output of feelings and unbidden thoughts of the subconscious neuroprocesses. It's just that we are aware of that output, while all other information exchanges are hidden from conscious view. Indeed, the processes interact in a complicated fashion and even change as part of that activity, as we see next.

5

Neuroprocess Hypothesis

According to the preceding chapter, an extremely conservative evaluation triggers the feeling of fatigue. It assumes that efforts will continue at the current level not just for hours, but for days.

Changing Fatigue

Athletes competing in long-distance races eliminate the unjustified evaluation with proactive deliberate thoughts that modify the subconscious fatigue neuroprocess.

That change is not easy since the fatigue neuroprocess is not directly accessible: The runner can only engage in deliberate thoughts that gradually replace the fatigue neuroprocess by a different one supporting perseverance.

The famous Finnish distance runner Paavo Nurmi put it thus:[32]

> "Mind is everything. Muscles are pieces of rubber. All that I am, I am because of my mind."

The feelings of perseverance propel the runner until the body reaches its physical limit. This happens in one of two ways:[33]

- The runner has calibrated the effort so carefully that she is at the point of physical exhaustion just as she reaches the finish line. At that moment, perseverance is overtaken by fatigue, and the runner collapses. But minutes later, she is up again and celebrating.

- If the runner has miscalculated and exhaustion sets in before the end of the race, that calamity manifests itself in the "Full Foster"collapse position[34] where the runner crawls on elbows and knees and finally collapses before or after reaching the finish line. Regardless of the case, survival is threatened.

The modification of the subconscious fatigue neuroprocess by deliberate thoughts isn't an unusual interaction. Let's look at another example.

Psychotherapy

In traditional approaches to psychotherapy, the therapist helps the patient understand the problem. The patient then acts upon that insight.

Cognitive behavioral therapy (CBT) is different. It is based on the postulate that thought distortions result in destructive feelings and behavior. Hence, the therapist helps the patient to think differently, with the effect that the patient abandons the negative feelings and behavior.

The key statement is:

> Our deliberate thoughts trigger our feelings, therefore changing our thoughts will change our feelings.[35]

CBT has proved to be effective for a variety of disorders, for example, depression, anxiety, alcohol and drug abuse, and eating disorders.[36]

Translated to the world of subconscious and conscious neuroprocesses, the main claim of CBT becomes:

> Deliberate thoughts of conscious neuroprocesses influence subconscious neuroprocesses. In particular, the deliberate thoughts change

feelings and unbidden thoughts produced by subconscious neuropro-cesses.

Two additional cases demonstrate the interaction of neuroprocesses.

Optimal Walking

For purposeful walking, a subconscious neuroprocess determines the optimal speed so that the destination is reached with minimal total energy consumption.[37] The neuroprocess outputs feelings for different speeds.

The optimal speed is associated with a feeling of comfortable achieve-ment while other speeds produce feelings of impatience or discom-fort. The neuroprocess determines the optimal speed within a few minutes of walking.[38]

We can readily change our walking speed from optimal to slower or faster values while ignoring the feeling of impatience or discom-fort.

For example, we may want to arrive sooner due to some commit-ment, and thus walk at a brisk rate. Or we may decide to slow down to a crawl, for example when we visit an art gallery. In either case, the goal we are pursuing with the changed speed provides a pleasant feeling that overrides the negative emotion arising from the nonoptimal speed.

Playing the Piano

When a piano virtuoso practices nine hours every day, she sharp-ens subconscious neuroprocesses that operate the fingers of her hands with lightning speed. During the concert, she doesn't con-sciously trigger each of these movements, but allows the neuro-processes to operate the muscles. Instead, she focuses on the mood and tone and flow of the music. In some sense, she narrates the story of the composition.

She must update these subconscious neuroprocesses daily since otherwise the precision of muscle control deteriorates.

Interaction of Neuroprocesses

Each of the above examples involves an extensive process connecting subconscious and conscious neuroprocesses.

In one direction, subconscious neuroprocesses produce feelings, trigger unbidden thoughts, and initiate direct actions. Except for some of the actions, we are aware of this information.

In the reverse direction, the actions, decisions, and deliberate thoughts of conscious neuroprocesses affect subconscious neuroprocesses. We see the effect indirectly through modified output of the subconscious neuroprocesses.

The exchange process isn't happening sporadically. Rather, it should be viewed as two rivers of information that continuously flow in both directions and change the neuroprocesses.

Model Building

The neuroprocesses don't just evaluate input, carry out reasoning, and produce output. They also build and maintain information on a huge scale. In this book, the most important aspect is that they create and use a vast collection of *models of the world*. These models *are* the world as far as the neuroprocesses are concerned.

Before the advent of writing, the teaching of elders enhanced the learning of models for the conscious neuroprocesses. Once writing was available, some models were stored outside the body and could be acquired by reading.

We view the models of the world to be part of the neuroprocesses in the same sense that a computer program may reuse internal data it built previously.

Neuroprocess Hypothesis

The following hypothesis—the *neuroprocess hypothesis*—states the two key features of the neuroprocesses established in this chapter.

The neuroprocesses change continuously. In particular, they modify each other.

The neuroprocesses consider the models *of the world that they create to be* facts *of the world.*

Errors

The neuroprocesses do not perform perfectly. Now and then they make mistakes, sometimes major ones. The following four aspects of the neuroprocesses are crucial for the analysis of such errors.

- The feelings and unbidden thoughts passed from the subconscious neuroprocesses to the conscious ones are the *only* information the latter processes obtain about the world. Indeed, as far as the conscious neuroprocesses are concerned, those data are *facts* of the world.
- Thoughts at the conscious level may change subconscious models.
- The conscious neuroprocesses cannot uncover why subconscious models have changed since they do not have insight into the workings of the subconscious neuroprocesses. At best, the conscious neuroprocesses can speculate why the output of the subconscious neuroprocesses changes.
- The extent and speed with which conscious thoughts change subconscious models depends on the intensity of the conscious thoughts. Higher intensity produces larger changes faster.

The next chapter shows that the neuroprocess hypothesis is consistent with the results of neuroscience.

6

Justification

Chapters 3–5 cite a number of results that directly or indirectly support the concept of subconscious and conscious neuroprocesses and the neuroprocess hypothesis. Complete validation demands more.

We must show that the concept is consistent with relevant results of neuroscience. It is a Herculean task since neuroscience has produced an ocean of results at both low and high levels of detail.

- Results at low level cover the behavior of *cells* and other elementary building blocks. Here are examples. *Grid cells* of periodic triangular or hexagonal arrays are part of the brain's metric for the representation of space. *Place cells* represent specific positions in space. *Head-direction cells* define the direction in which the head is pointed.[39]

- Results at high level concern *features* of the nervous system and their interaction. Example results link the perception of *events* and *memory*.[40]

Evidence

Three books summarize the parts of the theory connected with the neuroprocess hypothesis in exemplary fashion.

- *Livewired* by D. Eagleman[41] lays out the miraculous performance of the brain and, more generally, the nervous system.
- *Physical Intelligence* by S. Grafton[42] vividly describes the intricate web of connections linking, in the words of the book, "body and mind."
- *Emotional* by L. Mlodinow[43] lays out key results of *affective neuroscience*, which investigates the fascinating connection of subconsciously produced emotions and consciously made decisions.

The definition of the subconscious and conscious neuroprocesses and the neuroprocess hypothesis is consistent not only with the results described in these books, but also with the following material.

- *Feeling & Knowing* by A. Damasio[44] explains that the drive for survival produced the nervous system. One may rewrite the steps and obtain a story about the development of the neuroprocesses.
- *Breath* by J. Nestor[45] tells how breathing influences our well-being. The story can be recast using neuroprocesses.[46]
- *Thinking, Fast and Slow* by D. Kahneman[47] analyzes fast and slow thinking. Fast thinking can be viewed as part of unbidden thought output of subconscious neuroprocesses, while slow thinking is connected with deliberate thoughts of conscious neuroprocesses.
- *Full Catastrophe Living* by J. Kabat-Zinn[48] proposes *mindfulness* as a key tool for managing our lives. The meditation achieving mindfulness essentially is training of subconscious neuroprocesses by conscious thoughts.[49]
- The introduction to the National Academy of Sciences colloquium "Brain Produces Mind by Modeling" in 2019 includes the following statement:[50]

  "An intriguing possibility is that the brain produces the mind by forming a model of the entire environment including the body, the physical environment, other agents, and the social environment. It uses this model to learn, decide, attend, remember, perceive and produce action."

The intriguing possibility becomes a version of the neuroprocess hypothesis when we expand its single model to interacting subconscious and conscious neuroprocesses.

• In an entirely different approach, mathematical arguments mandate the existence of models in the brain.

"The living brain, so far as it is to be successful and efficient as a regulator for survival, *must* proceed, in learning, by the formation of a model (or models) of its environment."[51]

The reference doesn't assert any details about the models, for example, how they fit together or influence each other. But it supports the claim that the neuroprocesses build and use models of the world.

Summary

Ample evidence justifies the concept of subconscious and conscious neuroprocesses and the related neuroprocess hypothesis.

———————

We move on to Part II, where we investigate why AI projects succeed or fail.

Part II

Artificial Intelligence

7
Quest

Artificial intelligence (AI) creates machines for complex tasks such as the translation of one language to another, the medical diagnosis of illnesses, and the control of driverless cars. We meet a precise definition of AI later in this chapter.

During the past six decades, AI research has had far fewer successes than other areas of science that, over the same period, produced ever faster computers, a multitude of new materials, and rockets that brought man to the moon and back, to name a few of the outstanding results.

Indeed, one might reasonably claim that AI has produced impressive results only during the past three decades. Chapter 1 lists the following examples:

- The chess computer Deep Blue[52]
- The Google search engine[53]
- DeepL and Google Translate[54]
- ChatGPT[55]

How is it possible that the early decades saw little progress and that mistakes are still being made today, as demonstrated in Chapter 1? Is it extreme difficulty of the tasks, or is something else at work?

In this chapter we supply an explanation using results about the subconscious and conscious neuroprocesses. As we shall see, the stumbling block hasn't been the difficulty of the tasks, but a mistaken assumption about the way humans think.

To start, we clarify some concepts.

What is Intelligence?

The following statements demonstrate the wide-ranging use of the words "intelligence" and "intelligent":

- That's an intelligent question.
- She is an intelligent observer.
- Intelligence cannot be acquired.
- The IQ is a poor measure of intelligence.

One might say that each case associates some sort of cleverness or mental ability with the words "intelligence" and "intelligent."

We need a more precise characterization of intelligence that allows us to classify the performance of neuroprocesses. The predecessor book supplies the desired definition:[56]

> *Intelligence* is *demonstrated* by the neuroprocesses when they achieve their goals.

What does this statement mean? Take the driving of a car. The neuroprocesses governing the driving process have the goal of doing this well. At the same time, such performance requires considerable intelligence.

Hence, when these neuroprocesses achieve that goal, they implicitly have demonstrated significant intelligence. The same arguments apply to other difficult tasks such as inventing machinery, reading books, or flying to the moon.

Our definition also covers other evidence of intelligence, for example, the situation where neuroprocesses successfully protect the body from excessive physical effort or compute the optimal walking speed.

The definition even declares intelligence to be demonstrated at much lower levels of the body, for example, when a neuroprocess is the defensive action of bacteria against invading viruses.[57]

What is Mind?

There is a wealth of definitions of "mind." It includes an overall, vague declaration that mind is the collection of all faculties involved in mental phenomena.[58] In contrast, we defined previously:[59]

> Mind is the awareness of the conscious neuroprocesses as they take place. This includes awareness of the feelings and unbidden thoughts supplied by the subconscious neuroprocesses to the conscious ones.

The definition implies that the mind isn't an entity separate from the body.

What is Artificial Intelligence (AI)?

Prior definitions have been quite broad.[60] For example, AI has been declared to be the capacity of computers or other machines to exhibit or simulate intelligent behavior, and the field of study concerned with this.[61]

We employ a narrower, in our opinion more precise, definition that refers to intelligent behavior of subconscious neuroprocesses.

Let's see why this is important.

On the one hand, there are difficult problems that require considerable intelligence of the conscious neuroprocesses, but much less of the subconscious ones.

For example, the construction of equipment to fly to the moon demands knowledge of materials, physical processes, mathematics, and so on. Most of that information has been written down and is brought via subconscious neuroprocesses to the conscious ones, or is supplied by the subconscious processes from stored memory.

The conscious neuroprocesses carry out the difficult manipulation of that information, while the subconscious neuroprocesses play a supporting role. The engineers, mathematicians, and scientists involved in that research would strongly object if we classified it as an AI effort.[62]

On the other hand, when one translates English to German, the difficult part of the effort is carried out by highly intelligent subconscious neuroprocesses. It's almost like magic that these processes bring up entire sentences in the target language without conscious effort. Hence we would want language translation to be part of AI research.

We now define that AI research concerns precisely the problems that, when handled by humans, require substantial intelligence of subconscious neuroprocesses. That definition will not raise the hackles of engineers, mathematicians, and scientists, a pleasant side effect. But it also is broad enough that it captures all the projects AI should be interested in. This includes, for example, the composition of music and the creation of art.

Here is a compact statement of our definition.

> *Artificial Intelligence (AI)* is the research program concerned with the design and implementation of machines for tasks requiring significant intelligence of the subconscious neuroprocesses.

Note that the definition doesn't say anything about the level of intelligence of the conscious neuroprocesses, so that level could be anything.

Let's look at a specific case: Data analysis by *machine learning (ML)*. An important part of ML research concerns methods that identify structure in training data and use it later to classify additional data. Often, the learning process doesn't have access to any prior insight into the structure of the data.

Consider *nonparametric statistics*, an area of science that started in the 13th century CE.[63] It identifies structural information in given data without any prior knowledge, for example about the distribution underlying the data. Here, too, initial data are used for estimation. That insight is then applied to additional data. Sounds like ML, doesn't it?

Our definition of AI cleanly separates the two cases. Conscious neuroprocesses of significant intelligence have produced the results of nonparametric statistics, while ML has focused on problems requiring substantial intelligence of subconscious neuroprocesses. For example, an ML method may isolate persons in a photograph or quantify the intuition that a physician brings to medical diagnosis.

AI as Marketing Buzzword

"Artificial Intelligence" has become a buzzword in the 21st century. Marketing hype often labels some method as an AI technique and use words such as "intelligent" or "smart" when in reality the scheme if carried out by humans would require little intelligence of subconscious neuroprocesses.

Engineers, mathematicians, and scientists working outside AI are rightfully irritated when this happens since their methods and results are mislabeled.

The relabeling of traditional methods has had the effect that the early 21st century supposedly has produced a flood of wonderful AI machines and systems. In reality, many of these machines and systems have nothing to do with AI.

An example are the so-called *smart* thermostats. They are an engineering achievement to properly control temperature.

AI methods, in particular ML schemes, are now used in other areas of science, sometimes extensively.[64] These applications require significant intelligence of conscious neuroprocesses, but not of subconscious ones. Now and then people using the methods claim that they are *doing* AI when in reality they are *using* AI methods. An example claim: "[A] team ... has developed an artificial intelligence-led process that uses big data to design new proteins."[65] The term "artificial intelligence-led process" gives the vague impression that the team somehow carries out AI research. Actually, they are just using tools of that area.

AI Research

How can we carry out AI research? Specifically, how can we represent the activities of highly intelligent subconscious neuroprocesses in a machine? A reasonable answer seems to be: We construct guesses about the performance of these neuroprocesses and use that information as a guide.

How can we obtain those guesses?

Mind Observation

Here is one way. We envision instances of the given problem and use our mind—that is, our awareness of the conscious neuroprocesses and of the feelings and unbidden thoughts produced by the subconscious ones—to understand how we cope with these instances.

To this end, we slow down the mental processes to a snail's pace and look at each step in great detail. It's as if we observe ourselves thinking in slow motion under a microscope. Since we use our mind for this, we call the method *mind observation*.

As an example, suppose we want to devise a method for translating English to German. In the first step, we invoke mind observation.

For instance, we observe how we handle the English sentence

"The jeweler cleaned Sophie's necklace."

Slowing down the process, we discover that we first gain an understanding of the meaning and grammatical role of each word in the sentence. Then we move to equivalent German words: The word "jeweler" is connected with the German "Juwelier," "cleaned" becomes "reinigte," the genitive case "Sophie's" becomes "Sophies," and "necklace" turns into "Halskette." Finally, we combine the German terms to the desired German sentence:

"Der Juwelier reinigte Sophies Halskette."

We repeat the process for other sentences and become convinced that the above sequence of steps captures the essence of translation. We condense that insight to a process hypothesis. It guides us when we construct the desired translation machine.

Since we have used the mind to understand the translation process, we are convinced that the process hypothesis is correct and the resulting machine will function perfectly. After all, the process hypothesis captures the essence of the operation, doesn't it?

But then we apply our machine to the following sentence:

"Muhammad Ali cleaned Joe Frazier's clock."

It looks like the earlier sentence, doesn't it? The name "Muhammad Ali" has replaced "The jeweler," "Joe Frazier" has taken on the role of "Sophie," and "clock" stands in for "necklace."

Our machine then outputs the German statement

"Muhammad Ali reinigte Joe Fraziers Uhr."

Anybody familiar with Muhammad Ali's rout of Joe Frazier during three famous boxing matches in the 1970s will find the German sentence hilarious. The translator needs to know the fact that the colloquial English "clean one's clock" means to beat, thrash, or defeat somebody decisively. It stems from an early, now abandoned interpretation of "clean" as punching someone and of "clock" as the face.[66]

How do our subconscious and conscious neuroprocesses translate that sentence? The names "Muhammad Ali" and "Joe Frazier" prod subconscious neuroprocesses to refer to memories of the two boxers, their feud, and the boxing matches. That information determines the roles of the words "clean" and "clock" in the subconsciously produced translation. The subconscious neuroprocesses then output the perfectly translated sentence plus a vague flash of the memories to the conscious neuroprocesses.

Shortcomings of Mind Observation

Why has mind observation misled us so badly? Didn't we obtain a complete understanding of the translation process?

No, we didn't, for two reasons.

- Mind observation glossed over the role of the subconscious neuroprocesses. Very complex evaluations by highly intelligent subconscious neuroprocesses determined the meaning of the sentence in the given context. But mind observation only experienced the summarizing conclusions. For example, "cleaning" was interpreted as the removal of contaminating material.

- Mind observation gave us the erroneous impression that we had fully understood what happened at the subconscious level.

The combination of these two flaws badly impacted language translation projects.[67] Let's restate them for general AI research.

- *When we use mind observation in AI research, we ignore that the insight includes nothing about the inner workings of the highly intelligent subconscious neuroprocesses. We know the input of these neuroprocesses and the output of feelings, unbidden thoughts, and direct actions, but nothing else.*

- *Mind observation represents the operations of highly intelligent subconscious neuroprocesses by oversimplifying statements. At the same time, mind observation gives us the feeling that the naive interpretation is correct.*

Mind Observation as Cause of AI Blunders

We claim that the two flaws had a huge negative impact on AI research:

Mind observation has been one of the root causes of major AI blunders.

What a bold claim! Indeed, somebody may strongly object. After all, what could be more appropriate than mind observation to understand how the conscious and subconscious neuroprocesses work and interact? Maybe we just need to carry out mind observation more carefully?

The objection reflects the almost hypnotic hold that mind observation has on us when we try to understand our thinking. But that approach is fundamentally flawed: No matter how much we slow down mind observation, we won't gain an understanding of the role of the subconscious neuroprocesses.

What is the alternative to mind observation?

Alternative to Mind Observation

It depends on the case. Generally speaking, we should look at the input into the subconscious neuroprocesses and their output, and apply results of other areas of human thought—for example, mathematics, science, psychology, and philosophy—to determine an appropriate representation. This requires innovation and unusual ideas instead of mind observation.

For example, the four outstanding successes mentioned earlier—the victory of Deep Blue, the amazing results produced by the Google search engine, the impressive translation performance of

DeepL and the Google translator, and the sophisticated answers of ChatGPT—rely on approaches very different from mind observation.

- Deep Blue: So-called deep searches into the solution space of chess produce the outstanding performance.[68]
- Google search engine: Chapter 8 sketches the process.
- DeepL and Google Translate: The impressive results rest on recursive prediction of the next word from the entire source sentence and the already produced part of the target sentence.[69]
- ChatGPT relies on a huge database and an extensive training program.[70]

Cycles of Failure

The AI errors triggered corrections, of course. But during the first four decades, from the 1950s to the mid-1990s, the new approaches failed, too, triggering further corrections, and so on. Each of these cycles started with unjustified hype and ended with a period of disappointment and funding cuts called *AI winter*.[71]

We analyze some cases of mind observation to demonstrate its shortcomings, starting with projects of the first four decades of AI research. This is ancient history, of course. But those were simpler times, and the dissection of uncomplicated projects of that period produces an excellent understanding why mind observation fails.

We cover three cases: The early Lisp language in Chapter 8, the rise and fall of expert systems in Chapter 9, and the early Prolog language in Chapter 10.

8

A Perfect Language for AI?

Consider the following mind observation:

"To understand what's in a box, we open it and scan the contents. Next, we select one item and open it."

Let's break down the thought into small steps. The action "investigate box" consists of two sub-actions "open box" and "scan items". Next are sub-sub-actions "select item" and "open item." How should we represent these actions in a computer program?

To AI researchers of the past, procedural languages such as C, Python, C++, or Java seemed unsuited for that task: These languages knew how to add numbers but were unable to handle actions such as "open box" and "select item."

Hence the researchers looked for a different language where one could define actions in terms of sub-actions, which in turn triggered sub-sub-actions, and so on.

Lisp Programming Language

The *Lisp programming language* seemed the perfect candidate for this task since it relies on so-called S-*expressions*. These statements have the following format:[72]

```
(action ...)
```

The leading term, action, is the name of what is to be done. The subsequent part, here indicated by dots, has details about the action. A very simple example statement involving numbers is

```
(+ 21 54)
```

The action is +, that is, addition. The numbers to be added are given by the two entries 21 and 54. Hence, execution of the statement produces $21 + 54 = 75$. That value is assigned to the entire S-expression.

Instead of the data 21 and 54, we may specify other S-expressions after action. Within them we may position further S-expressions, and so on. Such repeated nesting is perfect for specifying sub-actions for a given action, then sub-sub-actions within each sub-action, and so forth.

Connection With Mind Observation

Let's link such nesting of operations to mind observation, say when we translate a sentence. We search a dictionary for the words of the given sentence, use rules of grammar, and so on, to achieve the translation.

Each step is some operation such as a search in a file or identification of a grammatical rule. We encode each step in an S-statement, with suitable substeps, and voilá, we have created a translation machine.

The encoding of mind observation in S-statements is such a natural process that Lisp became the preferred language for AI research. A popular textbook for AI from the mid-1980s put it thus:[73]

> "In the study of Artificial Intelligence the reason for learning Lisp is roughly that for learning French when you are going to France—it's the native language.

> "There are occasional programs in AI written in languages other than Lisp, but if one were to take, say, the 100 best-known

programs in the field, probably 95 would be in Lisp, and of the remaining five, four were written before Lisp was available on most computers."

Lisp Computer: the Explorer

The overwhelming use of Lisp in AI motivated Texas Instruments, Inc., or TI, in the 1980s to create the *Explorer*, a computer dedicated to processing Lisp programs.[74] TI manufactured the Explorer in large numbers, with two goals.

- The company intended to use the Explorer for planning and managing its own production. To this end, TI assembled an AI department of about 20 scientists with advanced degrees in diverse fields. An elite group, indeed.
- Beyond the use within TI, the Explorer was to become *the* computer for Lisp processing and therefore the universal tool for AI research.

TI launched a big push inside the company to promote use of the Explorer. Outside, intensive advertising aimed for large sales. Given the Explorer's impressive performance, the initial selling price was substantial.[75]

Failure of the Explorer

Within a few years, it became evident that the Explorer was a catastrophic failure on two fronts.

- The Explorer was distributed within TI but not used. People couldn't see how this machine would make planning or management any easier. TI eventually gave up and disbanded the entire AI department.
- The Explorer failed in the marketplace as well. People did not buy the machine even when the price was reduced. Eventually

TI shut down production and wrote off the entire venture. The total loss ran into hundreds of millions of dollars.

Current Use of Programming Languages

Let's contrast the mistaken idea of Lisp as *the* AI language with current use of programming languages for AI projects.

Google is one of the premier AI companies. The products range from the Google search engine to self-driving cars. The programming languages used by Google include C, Python, C++, and Java. According to the original AI philosophy, all of them are unsuitable for AI research. Why was that opinion mistaken?

Let's look at the Google search engine for an answer.

Google Search Engine

Search engines originally relied on mind observation, as follows. Suppose we want to find websites providing information about a topic of medicine, say infection. Using mind observation while we browse the Internet, we look at each use of the word "infection," read the context, and evaluate whether it is interesting information.

How is Google's search engine different?

Here is a nontechnical, simplified explanation.[76] Google scans all available websites and ranks each one by examining the rank of websites that refer to it. If this sounds to you like a definition of rank that refers to itself, you are right. But that seeming self-reference can be resolved by recursive scoring of websites.

When the Google search engine processes a query, it identifies the websites that contain answers, then outputs the information supplied by highly ranked websites.

Can you see that this scoring method is far different from any website evaluation based on mind observation? It doesn't decide whether a website containing "infection" has an explanation the user may be interested in, by reading and interpreting the text. Instead, it relies on the mathematics of ranking websites.

Procedural languages such as C, Python, C++, and Java are perfect for the task. The resulting Google search engine functions as if clairvoyant. It offers a few options to the user to make sure that it understands what the user is interested in, then supplies the right information.

Performance of Google Search Engine

How useful is the Google search engine? In 2022, it answered 8.5 billion queries every day.[77] Let's put this number in perspective. Suppose we have established a space colony on the moon and a spacecraft brings supplies to the moon on a regular schedule.

During each round trip, the spacecraft travels 477,800 miles. Suppose the spacecraft moves the ridiculously small distance of 1 foot each time Google answers a query.

How far does the spacecraft travel during one day? The answer: The spacecraft makes more than three round trips to the moon every day!

Lisp in 2022

Since those early days, researchers have developed 28 versions of Lisp.[78]

It no longer is the dominant programming language for AI as envisioned in the 1980s. Nevertheless, Lisp has been used in a number of applications; for example, for rule-based systems, music composition, aircraft analysis, autopiloting space craft, and scheduling.[79]

However, the fact remains that complex AI problems call for powerful procedural languages. This precludes the use of Lisp.

The next chapter shows how mind observation misled researchers to create AI software that at first was touted to be a major accomplishment but then turned out to be useless.

9

Expert Systems

Mary is a skilled weekend mechanic. She changes the oil of her car, replaces brake pads, and installs a new water pump. Indeed, she never has a repair shop work on her car.

The neighbors rely on her advice when they have car trouble. Here is a typical conversation.

Neighbor Sean: "The car doesn't start. What should I do?"
Mary: "When you push the start button, does the starter just click or does it turn the engine?"
Sean: "The engine turns over."
Mary: "When did you use the car last?"
Sean: "A week ago. I changed a tire in front of the garage, then drove the car back in."
Mary: "Water condensed inside the cylinders on the spark plugs after the very short drive. That's shorting out the spark plugs. Get in the car, depress the accelerator completely to the floor, and push the start button. It will take about 10 seconds for the plugs to clear. When the car starts, release the accelerator."
After a few minutes:
Sean: "Your suggestion worked perfectly. Thank you very much."

Construction of Expert System

Mary thinks that her knowledge should be encoded in software that people can access on the Internet. Then she wouldn't be called all the time. Even people she doesn't know could get help.

She uses mind observation to go over her calls with Sean and other neighbors, and encodes her insight into the functioning of cars in *rules*. For example:

```
IF starter_turns_over_engine AND car_does_not_start AND
earlier_short_trip
    THEN condensed_water_on_spark_plugs.

IF condensed_water_on_spark_plugs
    THEN run_starter_for_at_least_10_seconds.
```

She inserts the rules into an *expert system* that carries out the following steps. It asks the user for some initial information, then applies the data to every rule and checks if the IF condition is satisfied. Whenever that happens, the system stores the conclusion as additional knowledge.

Execution of Expert System: Chaining

As long as the system hasn't produced a conclusion that constitutes advice for the user, it asks for more information with the hope that the IF conditions of additional rules become satisfied.

The expert system stops when the process has established some advice.

The computational process is called *forward chaining*. There is an inverse process called *backward chaining* where some conclusion is postulated and the expert system works backwards from that conclusion to initial data. Here, too, the expert system asks the user for information to satisfy rules. But instead of searching forward using conditions of rules, it works backwards from conclusions.

Role of Mind Observation

The entire process is based on mind observation. It's what we be-come aware of when we observe ourselves thinking about car diag-nosis. Accordingly, Mary believes that the expert system will work very well.

AI researchers generally held that belief during the heyday of ex-pert systems in the 1980s and 1990s. There finally was a successful AI product, after all those failing AI systems of the 1960s and 1970s.

AI researchers also created *expert system* shells, for example CLIPS,[80] for the construction of expert systems. One only had to insert the rules since the chaining computations were built into the shell. AI researchers produced textbooks about expert systems, and univer-sities offered courses. It was a glorious period for AI.

Demise of Expert Systems

Then everything collapsed. By the early 2000s, publication of new books covering expert systems had ceased, and universities no longer offered courses on the topic.[81]

What happened? The process hypothesis based on mind observa-tion had turned out to be plain wrong. Chapter 7 tells why. We summarize that explanation:

> *The subconscious neuroprocesses perform sophisticated operations that the conscious neuroprocesses cannot explain. The latter processes hide their ignorance and offer vague statements about those operations.*

Here is an example. When Mary, who is a very skilled mechanic, is faced with a complex problem, she asks questions such as, "When did you last drive the car?" Where does this question come from?

If we ask Mary why she is posing the question, she likely says, "It's an idea I had when I thought about the problem." When we push for a more detailed explanation, she becomes evasive and eventually repeats, "I just thought it was a good idea."

Another example: When neighbor Sean suggests, "Maybe the problem is water in the gas tank," Mary pauses a second and says, "I don't think so."

If we try to find out the basis for her claim, Mary says, "I just don't believe that this is the problem."

These answers demonstrate that Mary relies on intuition when she analyzes car problems: Her diagnosis is correct, but she cannot justify the choice.

The rule-based expert system has no counterpart to Mary's ability to ask relevant questions and exclude useless speculation. Indeed, the system mindlessly asks for information, applies the rules, and repeats this over and over until it either stops with some advice or declares that it cannot find a solution to the problem.

When an expert watches that performance, they shake their head and grumble, "That's an irrelevant question to ask, I would never do that."

Later, they say, "I would be long done." When the system doesn't end up with any advice, they complain, "This expert system is really useless."

This single example explains the wholesale failure of rule-based expert systems.

Alternative: Mathematical Logic

Can we do better? Yes indeed, but we must abandon mind observation and use mathematical logic instead.

First, we must replace the rules by more complex statements with alternative conclusions. For example, when asbestos is discovered in a building, the removal of the asbestos must follow complex regulations created by the Occupational Safety and Health Administration (OSHA).[82] Here is one such OSHA rule and the equivalent formulation in logic:[83]

Rule: If the activity involves the removal of surfacing asbestos containing material, then the activity is of Class I or Class III.

Logic statement: IF fact(removal) and fact(surfacing_asbestos_containing_material) THEN fact(class_1) OR fact(class_3).

We then must learn how to draw conclusions from such statements. This can be done, but the computations are much more complicated than chaining.[84]

Theoretical Results Doom Rules and Chaining

You might wonder, though: Couldn't we replace statements specifying alternatives with equivalent rules having just one conclusion each? Yes, in principle this can be done. But the resulting rule set is huge and cannot be assembled let alone processed by a computer.

This restriction becomes indirectly evident when one tries to create a rule set with single conclusions. When the expert system processes example situations, there are always instances where the system cannot determine the desired advice.

In response, one adds rules to handle such cases. But the new version produces yet another defective performance, and one adds rules again.

Mathematics tells us that this correction process will never stop in our lifetime, or for that matter, during the lifetime of several future generations.

A second difficulty stems from the fact that the expert system may pursue useless avenues where it tries to establish conclusions that actually cannot be settled at all. This can be evaluated by appropriate computations that are far more complex than chaining.[85]

A third aspect of rule-based expert system is just as bad. The system may ask for a lot of information that later, when the advice has been found, is seen to be irrelevant. Mathematical logic has a cure for this, too. But it requires a solution technique that is even more complex than for the above case where conclusions are selected. The method determines if an answer to a question can ever be helpful.[86]

A fourth difficulty arises in situations where information can only be obtained at some cost. For example, a simple blood test may supply the answer for one variable, while expensive magnetic resonance imaging (MRI) is needed for another variable. The objective of the expert system is to obtain a diagnosis at minimum total cost. That aspect makes the already difficult computations even more complex. Clearly, chaining cannot handle them.[87]

Successful Approach

When one implements the four fixes,[88] one can construct expert systems that are far more sophisticated than those based on rules with single conclusions.

When an expert sees such a system in action, they comment upon each query by the system with, "That's what I would have asked, too." When the system stops, they say, "I couldn't have done it any better or faster."

Why wasn't that approach adopted and widely used? At the time the method was first published, around 2000, expert systems were widely considered useless, and the new results couldn't overturn that summary judgment.[89]

CLIPS in 2022

The CLIPS expert system shell is still available and used.[90] One explanation for survival is the fact that rule-based systems can handle very simple situations. But this does not include AI problems of any complexity, as discussed above.

The next chapter covers another major AI blunder.

10

A Second Perfect Language for AI?

In 1982, Japan's Ministry of Trade and Industry started a 10-year project to create massively parallel computers for logic programming. It became known as the *fifth-generation project*.[91]

Fifth-Generation Project

The hardware of prior generations of electronic computers had relied initially on vacuum tubes, then on transistors, and finally on integrated circuits. The software began with machine language, then advanced to assembly language and structured high-level programming languages such as FORTRAN and C, and finally to non-procedural high level programming languages such as Prolog.

The fifth-generation project was to be a technological leap forward. Massively parallel computers would execute Prolog programs for complex AI applications.

Let's analyze that ambitious goal.

Prolog Programming Language

Prolog represents a wealth of facts with compact statements. We will not adhere to the Prolog syntax here, but restate it in English using the IF ... THEN format of Chapter 9. We emphasize that for the moment we restrict ourselves to the Prolog of 1982. Later we look at modern versions.

The Prolog of 1982 relies solely on rules with a single conclusion, except that variables may occur.[92] For example, using the variable X we may have:

```
IF X is a cat
    THEN X is an animal.
```

Since the rule applies to all possible things that X may stand for, it actually represents a potentially huge set of rules: For each possible value of X, there is one rule.

Suppose we think about an AI problem and carry out mind observation. Given the expressive power of Prolog, we become convinced that we can represent all facts in that language. Hence, a computer processing that Prolog formulation should be able to think and reason just as we do.

There are two problems with that argument.

Limitations of Prolog

First, the Prolog statements may stand for millions of rules once we substitute for each variable X the possible instances and derive explicit statements of the possible cases. How can a computer cope with that many rules?

Well, Prolog doesn't really expand the specified statements to rules covering all instances, but invokes cases only as needed in the computation process. Nevertheless, that restriction may still admit a large set of rules. The massively parallel computer of the fifth-generation project was expected to handle these large rule sets.

The flexibility of Prolog doesn't eliminate the fundamental problems encountered by expert systems as discussed in Chapter 9. In fact:

- Alternative conclusions cannot be coded.
- Useless goals and irrelevant questions cannot be systematically avoided.
- Costs of data acquisition cannot be minimized.

Failure of Mind Observation

One may summarize this as follows: Mind observation misled the AI researchers of an entire country to believe that:

- Prolog could formulate any AI problem of interest, and that massively parallel computers could handle the implicitly huge formulations.
- Prolog was sufficiently powerful to represent all activities of subconscious neuroprocesses.

The arguments about expert systems in Chapter 9 prove both beliefs to have been mistaken. It is impossible for any massively parallel computer to assemble, let alone process a Prolog formulation that implicitly represents statements with alternatives. Also, mathematical results almost certainly imply that the chaining methods of Prolog cannot avoid the selection of irrelevant questions or useless speculation of outcome, or achieve minimization of the cost of data acquisition.

In hindsight it is no surprise that the fifth-generation project failed. Indeed, it did so after an extraordinary expenditure of money and manpower.

Prolog in 2022

During the past decades, researchers have developed 20 versions of Prolog that have greatly enhanced the power and capabilities of the language.[93] We cannot possibly cover the enhancements, but observe the following.

The chaining mechanism has been vastly expanded.[94] However, the computationally difficult problems of avoiding useless avenues and inquiries, including minimization of costs in that setting, cannot be easily accommodated.[95] But these difficult tasks generally arise when we strive for approximate representation of intelligent subconscious neuroprocesses.

We conclude that modern Prolog cannot be considered to be *the* programming language for AI. But it can play a role in concert with other languages such as C, Python, C++, or Java.

The next chapter describes an AI failure of the late 2010s that is also rooted in mind observation.

11

Watson Health

In 2011, IBM's Watson computer beat human competitors in spectacular fashion on the game show *Jeopardy!*[96] Surely there were other applications where a Watson-like computer could do better than human experts. In a bold decision, IBM built a medical advisory computer called *Watson Health* that was based on the architecture of Watson.

The computer was designed for two difficult tasks of medicine: reliable diagnosis of diseases and selection of safe and effective treatments.

But then the approach that had worked so well for the game show *Jeopardy!* failed so badly that IBM shut down the Watson Health project and eventually sold the software in 2022 at a huge loss.

Reason of Failure

How was that failure possible when all signs predicted outstanding success?[97] The story is too complex for detailed coverage here. We attempt a simplified discussion that brings out key aspects.

Watson Health processed a huge amount of medical information from journals and databases. The system assumed that the acquired data contained hidden rules, and that these rules could be applied to new patients. Accordingly, the information about each patient was matched against the implicit rules, which were then ranked for relevance. The implicit rules with high relevance produced suggestions for diagnosis and treatment.

Mind Observation

Nowhere in this process do we see any detailed connection to the neuroprocesses of the physicians as they arrive at a diagnosis and treatment. In fact, all considerations of physicians about prior cases reflected what the physicians *thought* about diagnosis and treatment, but not what their subconscious neuroprocesses actually *contributed*. That is, they were based on mind observation.

"Whoa!" somebody might object, "Why is that important?" We have two answers.

Medical treatment of complex diseases relies to a large extent on deep insight the physician acquires over years of training and subsequent decades of practice. That process develops powerful subconscious neuroprocesses that the physician depends on but cannot explain.

The result: The diagnosis and treatment are individual decisions for each patient, yet on the surface seem to depend on just a few patient data. In some cases, that simplistic view may suffice. In others, it produces wrong results. Too many wrong results doomed Watson Health.

The second answer is just a story. It drives home the point that experienced medical practitioners rely on the stunning performance of their subconscious neuroprocesses that they cannot explain.

It's a true story except that the names have been changed. Mr. Smith has come to the office of Dr. Miller, a cardiologist with decades of experience.

Mr. Smith has a vague chest pain that won't go away. Dr. Miller is sitting at his desk as Mr. Smith enters the examination room.

Mr. Smith: "Good morning, Dr. Miller."

Dr. Miller gets up and says, "Good morning, Mr. Smith. You are in the wrong place."

Mr. Smith (stunned): "Pardon me, aren't you Dr. Miller? I am here because of chest pain."

Dr. Miller: "Yes, I am Dr. Miller. But you still are in the wrong place. You should go to your dentist instead. "

Mr. Smith (now truly flustered): "I don't understand."

Dr. Miller: "You have an infected tooth. That's causing a widespread problem in your body that includes your heart. Your dentist can solve this."

One glance at Mr. Smith 10 feet away, and Dr. Miller diagnoses the problem. And that without any conscious thinking. A young cardiologist couldn't have done this. It is a supreme performance of subconscious neuroprocesses that Dr. Miller cannot explain. He just *knows* the solution.

––––––––––––

For the AI blunders discussed so far, mind observation leads to computer programs that supposedly mimic human reasoning but do not achieve that goal.

We now look at a different kind of failure.

12

Neural Nets

Machine learning is a large research area of AI that deduces information from data.[98] *Artificial neural networks, neural nets* for short, are one of the many inventions of machine learning. They were motivated by biological neural networks and have proved useful in numerous applications, for example, process control, game-playing, pattern recognition, speech recognition, and medical diagnosis.[99] We cover here a basic case that suffices for our purposes.[100]

Operation

In general, a neural net accepts an array of numbers as input, does some mathematical operations, and outputs another array.[101] For example, the input array may be data of a person such as blood pressure, pulse, temperature, and whether they have shortness of breath, are unusually tired, or feel nauseous. The output is the diagnosis that they are suffering a panic attack or an actual heart attack, or that neither case applies.

Structure

The net carries out the computations in *nodes* arranged in *layers*. There is always one *input layer*, one *output layer*, and any number of *hidden layers*. The nodes of the input layer are connected with the nodes of the first hidden layer, whose nodes are connected with those of the second hidden layer, and so on, until the last hidden layer is connected with the output layer. The input layer accepts the input arrays, while the output layer issues the output arrays. Here is an example with one hidden layer.

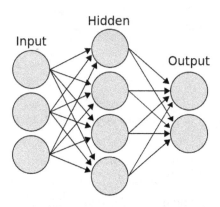

Artificial neural network.[102]

Initially, the user supplies a collection of input/output pairs. They are called the *training data*. Processing these data, the neural net learns via certain computations how to compute for each input the corresponding output. This step does not require human guidance.

Once training is completed, the neural net is ready to compute for any input—whether part of the training data or not—an output. An amazing machine, isn't it?

Accuracy

Suppose we have properly trained a neural net. Using statistical analysis, we can estimate how accurately the neural net will compute output for additional input data. But regardless of the case, we are always assured of the following attractive *training accuracy*:

For any input array that is equal to or very close to an input array of the training data, the neural net computes an output that more or less matches the corresponding training output.

By the very construction, the neural network is *consistent*: For identical inputs it computes identical outputs. This feature is attractive, but also has a drawback.

Faulty Action

Suppose the neural net controls a machine in the following manner. The input into the neural net is information obtained by the machine. The output then specifies the action the machine should take.

We abbreviate this description by saying that the neural net produces an action for each input.

Suppose for each input a large number of actions are possible. Some of them are safe, while others are dangerous. Can we train the neural net so that for each input it will always select a safe action?

At first glance, this seems possible. When we train the neural net, we select for each input case a safe action as output. Due to training accuracy we can expect that the neural net produces a safe action for each input of the training data.

But what happens when the neural net processes input data it didn't see during training? There is no guarantee that the action is safe. Hence we have:

Neural nets generally cannot select safe actions.

This limitation of neural nets is closely related to the inability of rule-based expert systems to select relevant avenues, as discussed in Chapter 9.

Surprised? The two cases seem really different, don't they? But mathematically they are in the same league of computational difficulty, and mathematical results about the complexity of these computations tell us that it is most unlikely that we will ever construct a rule-based expert system that dependably selects relevant questions, or a neural net that reliably computes safe actions.[103]

Summary

Neural nets are powerful tools in numerous settings. Their consistency is an asset as well as a liability: They cannot reliably compute safe actions.

The next chapter shows that neural nets play a central role in a class of AI blunders. You guessed right: The blunders are due to the fact that neural nets cannot dependably compute safe actions.

13

Action Observation

Recall that in mind observation we observe ourselves *think* in slow motion under a microscope. Let's define an analogous case where we observe ourselves *act* while slowing down time and focusing on every detail. We call this process *action observation*.

In the preceding chapters, mind observation misled AI researchers to design machines that supposedly could *think* like humans, but didn't. We now see that action observation can be similarly destructive.

We begin with a particular case: the driving of a car. The task clearly requires significant intelligence. Does this include highly intelligent subconscious neuroprocesses? Let's look at two situations we experienced ourselves.

Defensive Driving

We are driving on the main street of a small town. Some 150 feet ahead of us, a car has arrived at the stop sign of a side street. The car pulls forward a bit, say 2 feet. We react intuitively by moving the right foot from the accelerator pedal to the brake pedal. The other car accelerates into the street in front of us. We brake sharply to prevent a collision.

If we hadn't slowed down and put the foot on the brake pedal, we would have crashed into the car. In the jargon of driving schools, *defensive driving* saved the day.

Where did the cautionary action come from? The term "intuitively" provides the clue: Very intelligent subconscious neuroprocesses filtered from the traffic image the movement of the car on the side street and triggered the movement of the foot. Since we didn't react based on conscious reasoning, the movement of the foot was a direct action of subconscious neuroprocesses, as defined in Chapter 4.

Direct Action

A second example. We have driven a route in the city a number of times. As we move along today, we suddenly notice that the muscles of the arm turn the steering wheel a bit to the left. We are surprised and think, why on earth did we do this? A second later, a manhole cover comes into view. It is raised maybe 1 or 2 inches above the pavement, and driving across it would produce a nasty bump. Due to the slight movement of the steering wheel, the car straddles the manhole cover instead.

What triggered the muscles of the arm? Conscious thinking certainly didn't since we were surprised by the action. There is only one explanation: Highly intelligent subconscious neuroprocesses caused the action based on memory of earlier trips and the current position of the car. Evidently this is another instance of direct action.

Action Observation as Design Tool

Let's use action observation to design an autonomous car. We mount several cameras on a test vehicle and capture the views as we drive along a number of roads. Next, we design software that analyzes the vision data and identifies other vehicles, pedestrians, traffic lights, street signs, and so on.

In the laboratory we construct a car simulator that on the inside looks and acts like a car. Monitors shaped like car windows show the recorded views. We sit down in the simulator and drive the car, so to speak, and record all our actions. This is action observation. There are two types of actions: direct actions initiated by subconscious neuroprocesses, and actions decided by conscious neuroprocesses.

Neural Net

So far, we have collected the analyzed camera views and our driving actions. We designate the analyzed views as input and the driving actions as output of a neural net. We train the neural net using the collected data.

We install the neural net in a real-world car and add the software that analyzes the camera views. As the cameras record the views, the software recognizes other cars, pedestrians, and so on. The latter information is the input for the neural net, which passes the output action to machinery operating the pedals, turning the steering wheel, and son. In an abbreviated statement, we say that the neural net *drives* the car.

Evidently we have created a fully autonomous car. But have we really?

Road Test

We put the autonomous car on the road with a human driver who intervenes in case the system makes a bad decision. To our surprise, there are lots of interventions. For each one, we analyze why the error was made, add corrective cases to the training data, retrain the neural net, and start another test run.

Lo and behold, there are more errors. We fix them, too, test again, encounter more problems, and on and on. Why don't the errors ever stop? Why has action observation failed us?

Failure of Neural Nets

When humans drive, very intelligent subconscious neuroprocesses manipulate the views from the car. Indeed, they carry out complex evaluations and trigger various actions. In particular, they decide on safe actions as needed.

The neural net has learned some safe actions during the training process. But we know from Chapter 12 that the neural net is unable to select safe actions consistently.

For example, suppose the case of the driver on the side street was not part of the training program. When the autonomous car gets into that situation, it doesn't recognize that the slight forward movement toward the main road changes the driver from a polite and rule-observant person to an aggressive one risking an accident to get ahead.

The subconscious neuroprocesses account for this, but the neural net based on external views does not. As a result, there will be a crash.

As an aside, the crash will not be charged to the autonomous car since the other driver violated a traffic rule. This doesn't matter to you when you are a passenger in the autonomous car and suffer serious injury. What really counts is that defensive driving would have avoided the accident.

Enhanced Systems

The above conclusions still apply when neural nets are augmented by rule-based systems since the latter systems cannot reliably devise safe actions, either. The failure of the enhanced systems manifests not just in erratic actions but mayhem and death[104] or preventative shutdowns.[105]

Alternative Approach

To-date, the most successful company designing and testing autonomous cars seems to be Waymo, a subsidiary of Google. The control system is called *Waymo Driver*. The company doesn't reveal details of the technology but sketches general features. In particular:[106]

> "The Waymo Driver takes the information it gathers in real time, as well as the experience it has built up over its 20+ million miles of real world driving and 20+ billion miles in simulation, to anticipate what other road users might do. It understands how a car moves differently than a cyclist, pedestrian, or other object, and then predicts the many possible paths that the other road users may take, all in the blink of an eye.
>
> "The Waymo Driver takes all of this information—from its highly-detailed maps, to what objects are around and where they might go—and plans the best action or route to take. It instantly determines the exact trajectory, speed, lane, and steering maneuvers needed to behave safely throughout its journey."

The planning approach avoids the pitfalls of control exerted by neural nets and rule-based systems. Indeed, when the car faces the earlier-described situation of the driver rushing in from a side street, it has had experience about such an event and reacts in defensive fashion.

Elusive Perfection

Is Waymo Driver the perfect solution? Not knowing the technology developed by Waymo, we can only venture a guess. But from the above description, we are tempted to claim that the answer is no and more needs to be done.

Here is a scenario. We are driving on a two-lane access road for a freeway. We are in the right lane, have just passed an exit ramp, and want to move to the left lane and enter the upcoming entrance ramp.

In the left rear-view mirror we see a car come off the exit ramp at a speed substantially higher than ours. We turn on the left blinker. Should we veer into the left lane, trusting that the other driver will reduce the speed to the legal limit of the access road, or will they barrel onward?

To answer this question, we must evaluate what the driver of that car might think when they see our left-turn signal. From a mathematical point of view, this requires complex computations that cannot be carried out by a neural net or a rule-based system.

The triple-level process of "we evaluate what the other driver might think when they see our action" is difficult to implement on a computer. At the same time, it takes place almost continuously in dense traffic situations.

For example, we have a special approach when we see a car with a "Driving School" sign. For that case, we carry out different computations that take the inexperience of the driver into account.

In general, we even consider car models in our evaluation. For some of them, we anticipate that the driver is daring, while for others we assume the driver to be conservative.

Ethics

Up to this point we have ignored questions of ethics. They arise, for example, when a traffic situation leaves only bad choices.

A child chases after a ball into the street. Pedestrians are on the sidewalks. Cars are parked on both sides of the street, with some open spaces between them. We are traveling toward the child at 25 mph and cannot possibly stop in time.

All choices of evasive action are bad. The least bad of them is steering hard to the right into a gap between two parked cars while fully slamming on the brakes. Due to ABS (= anti-lock braking system), the brakes will not lock up the wheels, and the car will turn to the right as intended and hit a parked car at reduced speed, say 15 mph.

Air bags in our car will deploy. We will suffer some bruises but will survive. Both cars will be badly damaged. But the child will be unharmed.

How would an autonomous car work out all possible plans, decide which is least harmful, and implement it in time? How would the system account for harm to the child versus to us?

Much remains to be done, doesn't it?

General Case

Suppose human execution of a task requires highly intelligent subconscious neuroprocesses, and that somebody has designed a system for the task based on action observation. We claim that the system is virtually guaranteed to fail. The above discussion proves this for certain self-driving cars. But why does it hold in general?

Action observation links the input for the task with the observed human actions in the same way that a function in mathematics converts values of one domain consistently to values of another one.[107]

Action observation claims that a direct implementation of the function suffices, for example, using neural nets and rule-based systems. We show that any direct implementation is flawed.

Suppose the system encounters situation X. The system perceives X by certain sensors, which extract from X some information Y. The system regards Y as input and in straightforward computations selects action Z. In summary: X becomes input Y and then action Z.

When a person is in situation X, the highly intelligent subconscious neuroprocesses perceive more than the system-sensed Y. The neuroprocesses also supplement X with data from a vast storehouse of memory.

Next, the subconscious neuroprocesses carry out complex computations that, together with the results of conscious neuroprocesses, result in appropriate action.

In the fortuitous case, that action more or less matches the system-computed Z. But the action may also be quite different. In the latter case, the effect of the error may range from insignificant to catastrophic.

Evidently, no amount of error correction of the simplistic implementation can cure this flaw.

Summary

The chapters so far have established the following:

> *Any system that supposedly solves an AI problem is virtually guaranteed to fail if its construction relies on mind or action observation.*

———————

Another misconception besides mind and action observation has produced major errors in AI research. We need some background about language before we can get into details. The next chapter provides that material.

14
Structure of Language

We describe an erroneous theory about language. You may wonder: How can this be relevant for AI research? The answer consists of three parts:

- In 1921, Ludwig Wittgenstein (1889–1951) published a theory of language.
- In the second part of the 1920s, Wittgenstein realized that the theory was not correct.
- Over decades, many AI researchers proceeded in their work as if key ideas of the theory were correct. Some still do so today. Yet, all conclusions that rely on the theory are wrong.

We establish the gist of Wittgenstein's theory in this chapter, including a brief proof that it is wrong. In the next chapter we describe how AI research failed when it relied on the theory.

Let's start.

Wittgenstein's Landmark Books

Wittgenstein created two landmark books that address the following question: Is there a reliable, possibly time-consuming method to identify philosophical statements that actually are nonsense?

The first book was the *Tractatus Logico-Philosophicus*,[108] *Tractatus* for short, and the second one the *Philosophical Investigations*.[109]

The *Tractatus* is an amazing attempt to establish what language can and cannot express. The *Philosophical Investigations* supplies a powerful method for the analysis of philosophical statements and questions.

In our opinion, the depth and profundity of these works and the books compiled later from Wittgenstein's notes establish him as the greatest philosopher of the 20th century.

Failure of the Tractatus

Wittgenstein published the *Tractatus* in 1921. In the second half of the 1920s, Wittgenstein realized that the *Tractatus* contained "grave mistakes" (German *schwere Irrtümer*) that could not be remedied.[110]

Essentially, the *Tractatus* did eliminate inappropriate—for example, metaphysical—language, but also excluded legitimate communication.

The *Tractatus* includes two key ideas: *logical atomism* and the *picture theory*. We shall not attempt even a summary. Instead, we describe the main ideas of the *Tractatus* directly using a simple analogy.[111]

Description of a Radio

Suppose you are the curator of a History of Electronics museum. Somebody just donated a radio from the 1930s. You are curious what those radios were like. You remove the back panel and pull out the entire assembly. You get insight into the operation of this obsolete device in two steps.

First, you identify each component of the radio, such as the on/off switch, the transformer, the single vacuum tube, capacitors, resistors, and so on.

Second, you trace the wiring connecting these components. Then you write down statements. For example: "The vacuum tube is connected with ...," where you list the components; "The transformer is connected with the on/off switch", and "The vacuum tube is not connected with that switch." You might enhance the results. For example, you power up the radio and measure currents and voltages.

Detailed Results

Let's expand the investigation in a step that you couldn't do, but that we can imagine. Engineers and scientists examine the radio and write down all statements one can ever make about the radio. The explanation process goes down deeper and deeper into details but eventually stops at some point. For example, a nuclear physicist comes to details where they describe the behavior of electrons and muons but are unable to add anything else about these smallest particles.

Let's call all these statements the *detailed results* for the radio.

Consistency of Description with Detailed Results

Any statement that you have derived from the examination of the radio in some sense is *logically consistent* with the detailed results. For example, "The vacuum tube isn't connected with the on/off switch" is consistent with the detailed result that the vacuum tube would be destroyed if the high voltage at the on/off switch was applied.

From the Radio to the World

We use the above results about the radio in an analogy to explain the *Tractatus*'s view of the role of language in the world.

- The radio corresponds to the world.

- Each component of the radio corresponds to a thing of the world, for example, a house, a car, a tool, and a book, but also the color red, and even a pain we feel.

- The names for the components of the radio correspond to the words with which we refer to the things of the world.

- Statements about the components of the radio correspond to statements about the things of the world.

- The detailed results about the radio correspond to the facts connecting the things of the world. The arrangement is top-down. At the bottom are *atomic facts* where the things have names but no properties. We call the collection of these facts the *web of facts* of the world.

- The term "conceptually consistent" replaces the earlier used "logically consistent." It is defined as follows. A sentence is *conceptually consistent* with the web of facts if it makes sense within that framework. This doesn't mean that the sentence must be true. For example, the statement "The moon of the earth lies outside the solar system" can be interpreted in the web of facts but is false. On the other hand, the statement "Rome lies east of voltage" doesn't make sense since it links the city of Rome with a concept of electricity in an incomprehensible manner. Hence the sentence isn't conceptually consistent with the web of facts.[112]

Web Claim

We summarize the main ideas of the *Tractatus* in one comprehensive statement that we call the *web claim*. It links the web of facts with the things of the world and defines the meaningful statements that can ever be made about the world.

We focus here on meaningful statements since they are relevant for the subsequent discussion linking the *Tractatus* and AI research.

We ignore all other concepts of the *Tractatus* about statements, for example, the case where a statement is nonsensical.[113]

> *Web Claim:*
> *The world is completely characterized by a web of facts that specifies how the things of the world are connected.*
> *Any statement about the world is meaningful if and only if it is conceptually consistent with the web of facts.*

Limit of Meaningful Statements

The web claim implies that meaningful statements cannot go beyond the world in the sense that they cannot step outside the web of facts. Hence, meaningful statements can only indirectly *show* what the world is but cannot directly *say* that. This is a core conclusion of the *Tractatus*. It's a bit like the following. A clock *shows* the time but cannot *tell* what the nature of time is.

The conclusion creates a fundamental problem: The *Tractatus* contains a large number of statements beyond the world. For example, it characterizes what we call here the web of facts. Yet the *Tractatus* claims that such statements are not meaningful.

Wittgenstein attempts to resolve this contradiction with a famous ladder statement where he compares reading the *Tractatus* with climbing a ladder. The reader throws the ladder away upon achieving the desired insight.[114]

Proof that the Tractatus is Not Correct

Wittgenstein realized in the second part of the 1920s that the theory of the *Tractatus* did not cover certain cases of meaningful communication and thus was not correct.[115]

The neuroprocess hypothesis supports a short proof of that conclusion, as follows. The hypothesis states that the subconscious and conscious neuroprocesses rely on *models* of the world. Hence the models may differ from person to person. In fact, they often do, as discussions reveal.

This implies that human communication doesn't rely on a fixed web of facts. On top, the neuroprocesses continuously influence each other and change, and thus modify models all the time.

These conclusions falsify the *Tractatus*, which implies that the web claim is false, too. We record this below.

> *The web claim is false.*

Suppose a computer acts as if the web claim was true. We claim that the performance of the computer has a limit, as follows:

> *Computer limit:*
> *No computer that assumes the web claim to be true and acts accordingly, can process statements about the world as humans do.*

Indeed, as we have seen, humans reason on the basis of ever-changing models of the world, while the computer assumes, and argues within, a fixed environment of web facts.

The computer limit result remains valid for web claims other than the cited one, as long as the facts defining the web are immutable. We encounter such a case in Chapter 17. A finite collection of tables and rules then defines the facts.

The remainder of this chapter explores two tangential issues that you may skip. Hence if you like, you may jump ahead to the next chapter to read about the impact of the web claim and the resulting computer limit on AI research.

How Do We Communicate?

You may have the following question: Since the models of the world may differ from person to person, how do we know that any person can understand us?

The answer: We *don't* know this. When we tell a person something, we also operate neuroprocesses that anticipate the reaction of the person.[116] If the reaction agrees with the anticipated response, we assume that the person has understood the statement. If there is a different reaction, we clarify the statement. The exchange process stops when the person's reaction agrees with our anticipation.

If we cannot reach that stage in a few trials, we simply give up. Examples of frustrated final statements are "I don't think we can work together," "This isn't going to work out," or "Let's agree to disagree."

Wittgenstein's Subsequent Work

You may also have the following two questions: How did Wittgenstein proceed after the failure of the *Tractatus*? Is that subsequent work affected by the neuroprocess hypothesis?

The answer to the first question: Wittgenstein created a new way to solve philosophical problems in his masterpiece *Philosophical Investigations*. The book proposes that each person should resolve a given problem by investigating numerous settings that give rise to the problem. He calls the investigation of a particular setting a *language game*. Intensive exploration of the various settings via language games creates the desired insight into the problem.

The *Philosophical Investigations* as well as a number of books compiled later from his notes offer a huge number of examples of language games. In some sense, all this is training material. Upon successful study, the reader has become empowered to tackle any philosophical problem.

The neuroprocess hypothesis plus the main claim of cognitive behavioral therapy (CBT) explain why the method of language games is so effective. Indeed, the hypothesis says that the subconscious and conscious neuroprocesses rely on ever changing models, and CBT postulates that conscious thoughts can change those models. Thus, the extensive conscious thoughts of language games supply new insight via model changes.

A substantial part of AI research effectively adopted the erroneous web claim. The next chapter discusses one of the faulty outcomes.

15

Machine Translation

We have seen in Chapter 14 that the following claim is false:

> *Web Claim:*
> *The world is completely characterized by a web of facts that specifies how the things of the world are connected.*
> *Any statement about the world is meaningful if and only if it is conceptually consistent with the web of facts.*

The early history of natural language processing (NLP) is chock-full of AI errors due to adoption of the web claim. The language translation projects of NLP demonstrate this: AI research produced a variety of failing methods over a period spanning six decades:[117]

- *Rule-based machine translation (RBMT), from 1950 to 1980.*

- *Example-based machine translation (EBMT), from 1980 to 1990*

- *Statistical machine translation (SMT), from 1990 to 2015*

Each of the three methods is more sophisticated than its predecessor, but they have in common that they assume, more or less, that each word has well-defined meaning and thus can be translated by itself. But that assumption is just a much simplified version of the erroneous web claim, where each meaningful statement represents some facts of the world. Correspondingly, all three methods were a priori guaranteed to fail.

Neural Machine Translation

In 2015, a new method appeared: *neural machine translation (NMT)*. DeepL and Google Translate are examples. Each such method uses a neural net to construct from a given sentence the translated version as follows. It iteratively builds up the target sentence word by word. Each time it considers the entire given sentence and the translated string created so far.

Aren't NMTs still assuming the web claim?

Well, they do and they don't. They do since the translation process does not consider the setting of the entire text. But they don't in an artificial world where facts are defined by single sentences. Indeed, within that world, the translator attempts to find matches with the sentence to be translated, and out of this understanding creates the translated sentence word by word. As a result, each output sentence, seen by itself, makes sense and is grammatically correct, a huge improvement over the predecessor methods. Of course, manual postprocessing is still needed to correct inconsistencies among the sentences.

The next three chapters take a detour into the philosophy of AI. Each chapter covers a consequence of the fact that no computer that assumes the web claim to be true and acts accordingly, can process statements about the world as humans do.

16
Turing Test

The *Turing test*[118] is a test of a computer's ability to mimic human reasoning. We use the following version. A large box houses a human. A second large box contains a computer. An observer doesn't know which box contains the computer. To find out, the observer repeatedly provides information to the two boxes and evaluates the responses.

The computer passes the Turing test if the observer is never able to tell which box contains the computer and which the human. Alan Turing (1912–1954) asked:

Does a computer exist that passes the Turing test?

The question hasn't been answered despite decades of effort. We have the following partial answer:

No computer that assumes the web claim to be true and acts accordingly can pass the Turing test.

The proof uses the computer limit result of Chapter 14:

Computer limit:
No computer that assumes the web claim to be true and acts accordingly can process statements about the world as humans do.

Suppose a computer assumes that the web claim is true and acts accordingly. Due to the computer limit result, it doesn't process statements as humans do. Hence there exist inputs where the observer eventually realizes that one box does not respond as one would expect from a human and hence must contain the computer.[119]

Utility of Computer Passing the Turing Test

The discussion about computers passing the Turing test seems to imply that we really would like to have such machines. But isn't it possible that such computers are not that useful for AI research?

Let's investigate that question.

Suppose a computer has passed the Turing test. That is, the observer cannot tell which box contains the computer. The observer decides to ask some more questions, in particular, "Are you a computer?" The person answers, "No." The computer also answers, "No" since otherwise the observer would be able to identify the box containing the computer.

Next the observer asks, "Did you lie when you gave your previous answer?" The person obviously responds, "No." The computer follows suit with the same answer since "Yes" would reveal the computer's position.

At that time the observer still doesn't know which box contains the computer. But they have established that the computer has the intrinsic feature that it not only lies sometimes, but that later it also denies having done so.

One might argue that this is an isolated instance of obfuscation. To the contrary, it happens time and again. When the observer poses a computational problem, the human might say, "I need to use a computer to answer this in a reasonable amount of time." The computer will output something similar.

A computer says that it needs to use a computer? Crazy, isn't it? Would you want to use such a computer to solve AI problems? Not really.

The conclusion that no computer program that assumes the web claim to be true can pass the Turing test, has significant implications for philosophical discussions that have been going on for decades. The next chapter looks at a key situation.

17

Chinese Room

The *Chinese Room*[120] is based on a setting where a computer cannot comprehend Chinese symbols, yet processes inquiries formulated in Chinese and outputs responses in that language. The computer uses rules and tables to accomplish this. In effect, the computer processes the Chinese symbols just as some symbols for which it has no prior understanding, and totally relies on the information of tables and rules. Hence all information that can be derived from the tables and rules constitutes a web of facts for the Chinese world. The computer implicitly assumes that the corresponding web claim is true and acts accordingly.

Let's carry out a Turing test. One box has the computer and the tables and rules. The second box contains a Chinese speaker.

The main conclusion of Chapter 16, shown again below, proves that the computer fails the test.

> No computer that assumes the web claim to be true and acts accordingly can pass the Turing test.

Chinese Room

We convert the box containing the computer to the *Chinese Room* by replacing the computer by a human who manually carries out the steps exactly as done by the computer, without any additional thinking or reasoning. Hence the human produces the exact same output as the computer.

So far we have not mentioned one assumption underlying the Chinese Room: The computer supposedly has passed the Turing test. But we have seen that the computer cannot pass the Turing test. That contradiction implies:

The Chinese Room doesn't exist.

Based on the erroneous assumption that the Chinese Room exists, a number of results have been claimed during decades of philosophical effort.[121] Our conclusion invalidates the proofs of all those statements.

Numerous prior papers argue against conclusions drawn from the Chinese Room.[122] We shall not attempt to summarize the vast amount of material and say only that nonexistence of the Chinese Room permanently resolves the issue.

The next chapter covers another consequence of the Turing test.

18

Artificial General Intelligence

We consider an AI problem *solved* when we have created a computer that handles the problem just as competently as humans do.

The problem of *Artificial General Intelligence (AGI)* demands much more.[123] We are to create a computer that without any human guidance and thus entirely on its own understands any intellectual task and learns how to solve it. Let's call any such machine an *AGI computer*.

AGI computers ultimately make humans redundant. In fact, the computers might view humans as a hindrance to progress and decide to eliminate them. A frightening thought, isn't it?

Somebody may argue: This is just doomsday negativism. But consider the following: The reckless way in which humans have introduced some self-driving cars into urban traffic has resulted in mayhem and even death. Of course, this is not a major disaster, but indicative of human carelessness. On a larger scale, humans still conduct wars. Finally, humans are causing the extermination of a great many species world-wide. It's called *Holocene extinction* or *Anthropocene extinction*.[124]

If we would ask dolphins, whales, or elephants what they thought about us, they would declare humans to be a deadly epidemic that has befallen the earth.

Why wouldn't AGI computers installed in robots come to the same conclusion and set out to cure the disease by eliminating all humans?

We shall not pursue these depressing thoughts any further. Instead we investigate one technical aspect.

A Feature of AGI Computers

Somebody says that they have constructed an AGI computer. You feel that the goal has not been reached, but don't know how to prove your misgivings. The following result may help you make your case:

> No AGI computer assumes the web claim to be true and acts accordingly.

Let's prove this statement first and then use it. The proof is by contradiction. If an AGI computer assumes the web claim and acts accordingly, then according to Chapter 16 it cannot pass the Turing test. On the other hand, since it is an AGI computer, it handles intellectual tasks just like humans and passes that test.

Hence, if you can show that the supposed AGI computer relies on the web claim, you have demonstrated that it isn't such a computer.

———

During the preceding chapters, we have looked at a number of AI problems where the classification based on intelligent subconscious neuroprocesses is obvious. How can we carry out that classification in general? The next chapter suggests a method.

19

Classification Test

It's easy to see that the problems covered in Chapters 7-13 and 15 fall into the domain of AI: The solution by humans obviously requires considerable intelligence of subconscious neuroprocesses.

How about other cases? What constitutes evidence that a problem requires significant intelligence of subconscious neuroprocesses and thus can be classified as an AI task?

Classification Via Mind Observation

There is no easy answer since the subconscious neuroprocesses are by definition hidden from conscious inspection. But mind observation reveals symptoms.

The summarizing, deceptively simple description by mind observation contains fragments such as "... intuitively, it seems that ..." or "... past experience cautions that ...." These terms indicate that subconscious neuroprocesses carry out sweeping evaluations. Similar arguments apply to action observation when the AI problem calls for a machine that carries out certain actions.

For example, when we ask a chess grandmaster how they select the next move, they will talk about exploring the decision tree of possible moves and eventually say, "We cannot explore that decision tree deep enough to find the move for a certain win. Instead, we apply intuition to select what seems best."

Hence, playing chess is an AI problem. Really? How can that be when a six-year old child with a cell phone can beat a grandmaster?

We have stumbled upon a shortcoming of our test: We have ignored how much technical assistance a person is allowed to receive. Below we explicitly consider such assistance.

In the chess instance, the problem is no longer part of AI research when computer programs may be used.[125]

Another example. Writing an essay, say on the demise of the Roman Empire, is an AI problem. Not only must we assemble facts and evaluate them by logical arguments, but also must state our conclusions in a pleasing manner. Some of these steps require intelligent subconscious neuroprocesses.

Enter chatbots. We type "Construct an essay about the demise of the Roman Empire," wait a few seconds, and polish the resulting text so it looks like our own creation.[126] All this requires little intelligence of subconscious neuroprocesses.

A third case. We want to compose music. We sit at a piano, try a sequence of notes, think that this is not an interesting sequence; then try something else, and on and on. At some point we conclude, hey, this is the melody we are looking for. Lots of that thinking is intuitive and involves intelligent subconscious neuroprocesses.

Contrast this old-fashioned method with the use of music-composing computer programs. We push a button and seconds later have an entire symphony.[127]

Range of AI Problems

As we explore various problems for the need or non-need of intelligent subconscious neuroprocesses, it's fascinating to see how many problems at present pass the test and thus are part of AI research.

On the other hand, a tsunami of new machines is converting AI problems into simple ones requiring the push of a button. It's a revolution, plain and simple.

———————————

How can we avoid the AI blunders described in the preceding chapters? The last chapter attempts an answer.

20

Avoiding Blunders

When faced with a research problem involving human reasoning, we initially check whether it actually is in the AI domain. The first question therefore is: When the problem is handled by humans, does it require significant intelligence of the subconscious neuroprocesses?

If this isn't the case, we aren't facing an AI problem. Then mind and action observation, detrimental as they are for AI research, are excellent tools to get insight into the problem and potential solutions. For example, Operations Research—a research area started during World War II and still going on—focuses on problems requiring little intelligence of subconscious neuroprocesses, but much of the conscious ones. That area of research explicitly uses mind and action observation to develop models of operations and processes that are then implemented in computer programs.[128]

Suppose substantial intelligence of subconscious neuroprocesses is indeed required. Then we must make sure that we don't fall into the trap of accepting the web claim or using mind or action observation to understand the subconscious neuroprocesses. Let's see how we can accomplish this.

Web Claim

It's always tempting to adopt the web claim. After all, don't we fully comprehend what is going in the world around us and hence always perceive a portion of the web of facts of the world?

No, we must remind ourselves time and again, the neuroprocesses only operate *models* of the world. Worse yet, the models handled by the subconscious neuroprocesses are beyond conscious awareness.

Repetition of these reminders changes our attitude about data and their handling by the neuroprocesses. We no longer naively indulge in the belief of an objective world, but instead adopt a richer picture where each person functions on the basis of models that may, and often do, differ from those of other people.

Mind and Action Observation

The analysis of conscious neuroprocesses via mind and action observation has produced impressive results. Operations Research is just one of the fields of science that have created outstanding systems with that approach.

Given those success stories, one is always tempted to employ those tools for the interpretation of the highly intelligent subconscious neuroprocesses of AI problems. Yet, we have seen that this approach is virtually guaranteed to fail.

How can we escape the allure of mind and action observation?

The answer: We tell ourselves time and again that we simply don't know how the subconscious neuroprocesses accomplish their feats, and that we cannot obtain that insight by looking inward. The current partial results of neuroscience aren't of much help, either.

Instead, we must examine the input into these neuroprocesses and their output to the conscious ones, and strive to construct methods that approximately achieve that conversion.

A priori we have no preferences as to the kind of methods. For example, we may employ statistical schemes, neural nets, or logic machinery. In the third case, logic formulations handling complex settings—for example, formulas representing questions such as "Can the current traffic situation deteriorate into a pileup?"—are useful.

Avoiding the Traps

Most importantly, we must continuously be alert to the possibility that we are falling into the trap of adopting the web claim or using mind or action observation. It is upon us to check all the time whether this is happening, and then search for remedial action. The monitoring effort is comparatively easy, and we can do it with little effort. Much harder is finding alternate methods. In our opinion, that's the reason it is so difficult to achieve success in AI research.

We have come to the end of our journey. What have we learned?

Summary

Intuitive guesses about the performance of *subconscious neuroprocesses* are bound to be wrong. That's why mind and action observation virtually guarantee the failure of AI projects.

We are addicted to such intuitive guesses since they work very well, indeed are central tools, when we want to represent *conscious neuroprocesses*.

The faulty web claim, which declares the world to be completely described by a collection of web facts, is another tempting but wrong idea. Its source is the misleading everyday use of the word "fact." It does not refer to the world, but to a result of models about the world.

We can rid ourselves from the obsessive thoughts by systematic reminders of their falsity. Once we have achieved this, we can create methods that approximate the outputs of the subconscious neuro-processes.

The epilogue fits the conclusions into the broader setting of human investigation and reviews the results in nontechnical language.

Part III

Epilogue

In the 18th century, Leonhard Euler (1707–1783) created a vast body of mathematical concepts and results.[129] An example is his function concept. He declared each mathematical function to be a machine that accepts input of some domain and produces consistent output of another domain.

In contrast, AI researchers have produced over several decades a long list of erroneous results. The researchers still fail sometimes today, even with horrible results. An example is the mayhem and death produced by the erroneous systems of some self-driving cars.

What is the cause for that disparate performance?

Euler implicitly and sometimes explicitly relied on axioms that mathematicians in the 19th and 20th century made precise. Hence his results are permanent. In contrast, many AI results of past decades rested, and sometimes still do so, on speculation produced by mind or action observation and the faulty web claim about the world.

Here is a symptom of that massive failure: When the author started teaching AI in the 1980s, he was surprised that every year textbooks changed drastically. It was as if AI were being reinvented over and over.

Our recommendation for AI research then is very simple. We should explicitly accept that we don't know what the subconscious neuroprocesses are doing. With that admission, we are ready to look at the input into these processes and their output to the conscious ones, and then try to devise methods that produce for each possible input approximately correct output. We use whatever method of engineering, science, or mathematics is appropriate.

Nowhere should we claim that we are trying to represent *thinking* since it is a fundamental mistake to view the performance of the subconscious neuroprocesses as thinking.

During that research phase we temporarily ignore what the conscious neuroprocesses do. We always can understand them well using mind and action observation, as engineers, mathematicians, and scientists have proved for thousands of years. Hence we can readily construct schemes that convert the input of the conscious neuroprocesses into the desired output of decisions and actions.

The solution for an AI problem combines the methods for the subconscious neuroprocesses with the schemes for the conscious ones. Typically, we don't just concatenate the methods with the schemes where the output of the methods becomes the input for the schemes. Instead, we create sophisticated information exchanges between the methods and schemes, in agreement with the picture of Chapter 5 where two rivers of information flow in opposite directions.

One aspect surprised us when we worked out the main claims of this book. The *Tractatus*, Wittgenstein's wonderfully complicated yet wrong treatise about the meaning and use of language, is really important for the analysis of philosophical claims in AI.

Chapter 15 discusses the mistaken concept of the Chinese Room as a prime example.

We first formulated and used the concept of subconscious and conscious neuroprocesses in the book *Magic, Error, and Terror*.[130] With their aid, we showed how the neuroprocesses sometimes perform magic, but also can produce error, even terror, and what we can and cannot do about the latter two cases.

Later, we formalized the interaction of the subconscious and conscious neuroprocesses in the neuroprocess hypothesis and used it in the book *Wittgenstein and Brain Science*[131] to resolve philosophical questions that had been open for centuries.

This book is a third step: an analysis of the AI successes and blunders.

Isn't it amazing that the simple neuroprocess hypothesis helps unravel these difficult situations?

Notes

The notes frequently refer to the Wikipedia since it is readily accessible without charge. Unless otherwise indicated, it is the English version.

The entries of the Wikipedia often supply an extensive list of references for additional explanations. Pointing to the Wikipedia entry spares us from listing all those references.

Better yet, as insight into a topic grows, the Wikipedia changes as well. Hence the reader always obtains the latest information about the topic.

All links were verified in Spring 2023.

Chapter 1 Introduction

1. See Wikipedia "Deep Blue (chess computer)."

2. See Wikipedia "Google Search."

3. See Wikipedia "DeepL Translator" and "Neural machine translation."

4. See Wikipedia "ChatGPT."

5. See Chapter 11.

6. See Chapter 13.

7. [Ghorbani et al., 2019].

8. [Heaven, 2019].

9. [Dastin, 2018].

10. [Truemper, 2022].

11. [Kahneman, 2011].

12. [Chabris and Simons, 2011].

13. [Friston, 2010].

14. Section 7 [Friston et al., 2021].

15. [Truemper, 2022].

Chapter 2 Interaction with the World

16. [Kepler, 1627].

17. See Wikipedia "Orbit," "List of future astronomical events,"and "Timeline of the far future."

18. [Hawking and Mlodinow, 2010].

19. For example, we can share with others the visual impression of a house in the following sense. When we talk about the house, we know that others have the same or similar sense impression. But when we prick a finger, we cannot share the feeling of pain.

Chapter 3 Results of Neuroscience

20. See Wikipedia "Outline of the human nervous system."

21. [Eagleman, 2020].

22. Source: "Nervous system diagram." By Medium69, Jmarchn, CC BY-SA 4.0 https://commons.wikimedia.org/wiki/File:Nervous_system_diagram-en.svg, via Wikimedia Commons.

23. Chapters 1 and 4 [Eagleman, 2020].

24. See Wikipedia "Direct acoustic cochlear implant."

25. See Wikipedia "Enteric nervous system."

Chapter 4 Fatigue

26. Chapter 4 [Truemper, 2021] supplies part of the material of this chapter.

27. Craig Glenday, Editor-in-Chief at Guinness World Records, re-

ports on https://www.quora.com/What-is-the-longest-distance
-a-person-has-walked-in-one-go:
"Georges Holtyzer of Belgium walked 673.48 km (418.49 miles) in 6 days 10 hr 58 min, completing 452 laps of a 1.49 km (0.92 mile) circuit at Ninove, Belgium, from July 19 to July 25, 1986. He was not permitted any stops for rest and was moving 98.78 percent of the time."

28. p. 209 [Grafton, 2020].

29. p. 210, 211 [Grafton, 2020].

30. p. 213 [Grafton, 2020].

31. [Bennett and Hacker, 2022] has a far more detailed formulation. For example, the book describes a variety of feelings such as sensations, tactile perception, appetites, affections, felt desires, and obsessions. We do not differentiate among them here, except that now and then we refer to emotions. The book links the numerous concepts with physical processes. We skip this entirely.
We should mention, though, that the subconscious neuroprocesses encompass more than the processes investigated in the cited book. They include, for example, the control of heart and lungs, even the defensive actions of bacteria against invading viruses.

Chapter 5 Neuroprocess Hypothesis

32. See Wikipedia "Paavo Nurmi."

33. p. 214 [Grafton, 2020].

34. [Gibson et al., 2013] describes three stages of collapse.
- During the early stage—the "Early Foster" collapse position— the runner exhibits unstable gait and lowers the head.
- The gait deteriorates to a shuffle in the "Half Foster" collapse position, with head parallel to the ground.
- In the final stage—the "Full Foster" collapse position—the runner crawls on the ground on elbows and knees and finally collapses before or after reaching the finish line.

The reference conjectures that the collapse positions are indicative of a final, likely primordial, protective mechanism.

35. [Burns, 2020] provides not only a clear introduction, but is sufficiently detailed for readers who are looking for solutions they can

implement by themselves.

36. See Wikipedia "Cognitive behavioral therapy." For treatment examples, see [Beck et al., 1979], [Burns, 2008], and [Burns, 2020]. Chapter 3 [Truemper, 2021] describes a composite case.

37. See Wikipedia "Preferred walking speed." The total energy consumption per mile is called *gross cost of transport*.

38. [Selinger et al., 2015]. See also p. 192 [Grafton, 2020] and the section on Energetics of Wikipedia "Preferred walking speed." Chapter 6 [Truemper, 2021] compares the process with the difficult computation of optimal glide speed for airplanes.

Chapter 6 Justification

39. See Wikipedia "Grid cell," "Place cell," and "Head-direction cell." To learn more about the discoverers of these cells, see Wikipedia "Edvard Moser, "John O'Keefe (neuroscientist)," and "James B. Ranck Jr."

40. [Zacks, 2020].

41. [Eagleman, 2020].

42. [Grafton, 2020].

43. [Mlodinow, 2022].

44. [Damasio, 2021].

45. [Nestor, 2020].

46. Chapter 5 [Truemper, 2021] has details using the terminology of models instead of neuroprocesses.

47. [Kahneman, 2011].

48. [Kabat-Zinn, 1990].

49. Chapter 7 [Truemper, 2021].

50. See http://www.nasonline.org/programs/nas-colloquia/com pleted_colloquia/brain-produces-mind-by.html.

51. [Conant and Ashby, 1970] establishes that every good regulator of a system must be a model of that system. The stated claim about the brain is a corollary.

Chapter 7 Quest

52. See Wikipedia "Deep Blue (chess computer)."

53. See Wikipedia "Google Search."

54. See Wikipedia "DeepL Translator" and "Neural machine translation."

55. See Wikipedia "ChatGPT."

56. p. 3 [Truemper, 2022].

57. [Damasio, 2021].

58. See Wikipedia "Mind."

59. p. 3 [Truemper, 2022].

60. See Wikipedia "Artificial intelligence."
[Russell and Norvig, 2010] compares four distinct definitions of AI that cover—in the terminology of the reference—thinking humanly versus rationally, and acting humanly versus rationally. For each case, they quote representative formulations.

61. See Oxford English Dictionary "artificial intelligence." Stanford Encyclopedia of Philosophy "Artificial Intelligence" supplies an expansive discussion.

62. Here is a second, detailed example where conscious neuroprocesses perform difficult tasks while subconscious neuroprocesses play a supporting role. Operations Research started during World War II and is still going on. See Wikipedia "Operations research." Researchers in that area have made outstanding contributions to the operation of the economy. For example, for:

- Scheduling personnel and equipment
- Delivering packages
- Managing electric grids
- Scheduling production
- Routing vehicles
- Controlling traffic
- Scheduling public transportation

Researchers developed new areas of mathematics and expanded

existing ones to handle these tasks. For example, they originated or expanded:

- Linear, nonlinear, integer, dynamic, geometric, and stochastic programming
- Graph and network analysis
- Game theory
- Combinatorics
- Queuing theory
- Inventory theory
- Event simulation

No matter what task of the economy one considers, almost surely some Operations Research project has created efficient execution for at least a portion of the task.
Human handling of the tasks would require extraordinary intelligence of conscious neuroprocesses but little intelligence of the subconscious ones.
Accordingly, the standard AI definition would classify the problems tackled by Operations Research to be part of AI, while our definition would not. The researchers who carry out the work would agree with us that this isn't AI research.

63. See Wikipedia "Nonparametric statistics."

64. For example, the survey paper [Mowbray et al., 2021] demonstrates the extensive application of AI methods in biochemical engineering.

65. E. Ayshford, "Machine learning reveals recipe for building artificial proteins," *uchicago news*, 24 July 2020, https://news.uchicago.edu/story/machine-learning-reveals-recipe-building-artificial-proteins.

66. Two translators that according to 2022 valuation are excellent, fall into the same trap. Google Translate converts
    "Muhammad Ali cleaned Joe Frazier's clock"
to
    "Muhammad Ali putzte Joe Fraziers Uhr"
while DeepL offers
    "Muhammad Ali reinigte Joe Frazier's Uhr."
Since the German "putzen" is a synonym for "reinigen," the two sentences have the same, laughably false, meaning.
Even ChatGPT, a chatbot introduced by OpenAI in late 2022, fails

the test with
      "Muhammad Ali hat Joe Fraziers Uhr aufgeräumt"
A word of caution: Given the rapid progress in translators, by the
time you acquire this book, any one of these systems may produce
an appropriate translation.

67. See Wikipedia "Machine translation."

68. See Wikipedia "Deep Blue (chess computer)."

69. See Wikipedia "Neural machine translation." When one strips
away the mathematics from the neural methods and looks for the
ultimate reason of the excellent performance, one finds an explanation in the philosophy of Ludwig Wittgenstein (1889–1951). In
[Wittgenstein, 1958] he used so-called language games to show con-
vincingly that each word lives in a number of different environments. In some sense, the neural methods aim for a partial characterization of these environments. For additional aspects of language games, see Chapter 14.
For example, prior to the neural methods, the English sentence "I
am home, honey!" was translated to the silly German sentence "Ich
bin zu Hause, Honig!" It erroneously assumed that "honey" referred to the sweet viscous substance, and translated it to "Honig."
In 2022, DeepL and Google Translate produce the correct "Ich bin
zu Hause, Schatz!" They correctly interpret the English "honey" as
"darling," and use the appropriate "Schatz" (= treasure).
To be sure, these top-tier translators still can produce major errors, as we saw earlier for the example sentence "Muhammad Ali
cleaned Joe Frazier's clock."

70. See Wikipedia "ChatGPT." ChatGPT is by no means perfect. It
sometimes commits significant errors.

71. See Wikipedia "AI winter" and "Artificial Intelligence."

Chapter 8 A Perfect Language for AI?

72. See Wikipedia "Lisp (programming language)" for the history
of the Lisp language. Actually, there isn't just one such language.
Over the past 65 years, a total of 28 versions have been created. During the midpoint of that period, in 1994, a version called Common
Lisp was declared to be the standard.

73. p. 33 [Charniak and McDermott, 1985].

74. See Wikipedia "TI Explorer."

75. We have been unable to obtain the exact initial selling price, but recall that it was tens of thousands of dollars, a substantial sum in the 1980s.

76. For details about the Google search engine, see Wikipedia "Google Search."

77. Google does not publish how many searches it handles per day. In fall 2022, various websites estimated 8.5 billion searches per day.

78. See Wikipedia "Lisp (programming language)."

79. Wikipedia "Common Lisp" provides an expansive list of applications.

Chapter 9 Expert Systems

80. See Wikipedia "CLIPS."

81. For a detailed account of the rise and fall of expert systems, see Wikipedia "Expert system."

82. See Wikipedia "Occupational Safety and Health Administration."

83. Fig. 6 [Straach and Truemper, 1999] displays this and other rules of OSHA for asbestos removal. Each rule involves alternative conclusions.

84. See Wikipedia "First-order logic." Mathematically speaking, the formulation involves statements in first-order logic with a finite universe. Evaluation requires solution of the satisfiability problem of propositional logic (SAT). Unless the two complexity classes P and NP are identical, a most unlikely fact, procedures such as chaining will forever be unable to efficiently solve SAT instances.

85. Deciding whether it is fruitless to try and prove that a certain conclusion can ever be established, requires an answer to the following question: "Can there ever be information for the currently unknown variables such that a selected conclusion can be proved?" This question is at the second level of the polynomial hierarchy and hence very difficult. See Chapter 4 [Truemper, 2004] for details and Wikipedia "Polynomial hierarchy" for the mathematical background of the hierarchy.

86. The formulation of the question "Will information for this variable ever be useful to prove a given conclusion" is at the third level of the polynomial hierarchy. Solution methods are far more complicated than chaining. See Chapter 4 [Truemper, 2004] for details and Wikipedia "Polynomial hierarchy" for the mathematical background of the hierarchy.

87. Chapter 4 [Truemper, 2004] covers the cases where acquisition of values for variables entails costs.

88. See Chapter 10 [Truemper, 2004] and the references cited there. The chapter describes the construction of expert systems that allow for alternative conclusions. The systems determine relevant questions and avoid the pursuit of useless conclusions.
The formulation not only requires solution of the satisfiability problem of propositional logic (SAT), but also of problems at the second and third level of the polynomial hierarchy, including the consideration of costs. Unless that hierarchy collapses due to future mathematical insight—a most unlikely event—chaining cannot ever solve these instances with reasonable computational effort.
[Straach and Truemper, 1999] describes an example application.

89. Wikipedia "Expert system" doesn't even mention these results.

90. See "CLIPS, A tool for building expert systems" at https://clipsrules.net/.

Chapter 10 A Second Perfect Language for AI?

91. See Wikipedia "Fifth Generation Computer Systems."

92. [Merritt, 1989] provides a clear and elegant description of Prolog of the 1980s.

93. See Wikipedia "Prolog."

94. Alternative conclusions, default rules, constraints, and more can now be handled; see, for example, [Wielemaker et al., 2021].

95. As noted in Chapter 9, the problems of avoiding useless avenues and inquiries are at the second and third level of the polynomial hierarchy. They become even more difficult when costs are to be minimized.

Chapter 11 Watson Health

96. See Wikipedia "IBM Watson."

97. This section is mostly based on the detailed story of Watson Health's failure described in [Strickland, 2019]. See also Wikipedia "Merative."

Chapter 12 Neural Nets

98. See Wikipedia "Machine learning."

99. See Wikipedia "Neural networks."

100. Wikipedia "Types of artificial neural networks" supplies a summary of the neural networks.

101. For a summary of the operations of neural nets, see Wikipedia "Neural Network."

102. Source: "Artificial neural network" By en:User:Cburnett - This W3C-unspecified vector image was created with Inkscape, CC BY-SA 3.0, https://en.wikipedia.org/wiki/Artificial_neural_netw ork#/media/File:Artificial_neural_network.svg.

103. Selection of safe actions is a problem at the second level of the polynomial hierarchy, just as choice of relevant avenues is for expert systems. See Wikipedia "Polynomial hierarchy" for the mathematical definition of the hierarchy.

Chapter 13 Action Observation

104. In 2019 around 10 pm, a self-driving Uber car hit and killed a woman when the system didn't anticipate that pedestrians may jaywalk. NBC News Nov. 9, 2019, 2:28 PM CST, report by Phil McCausland: The automated car lacked "the capability to classify an object as a pedestrian unless that object was near a crosswalk," an NTSB report said. https://www.nbcnews.com/tech/tech-news/sel f-driving-uber-car-hit-killed-woman-did-not-recognize-n107 9281
Erratic actions of a self-driving Tesla are reported by Cade Metz, Ben Laffin, Hang Do Thi Duc, and Ian Clontz, "What Riding in a Self-Driving Tesla Tells Us About the Future of Autonomy," New York Times November 24, 2022, https://www.nytimes.com/intera

ctive/2022/11/14/technology/tesla-self-driving-flaws.html.
Misleading representation of the capabilities of Tesla's Full-Self-Driving technology is covered by Russell Mitchell, "Tesla says its self-driving technology may be a 'failure' but not fraud," Los Angeles Times December 8, 2022, https://www.latimes.com/business/story/2022-12-08/tesla-lawsuit-full-self-driving-technology-failure-not-fraud. According to the report, the Tesla website still included a doctored demonstration video, "done in multiple takes, with the driving system's failures removed, including a crash into a fence."
The following website supplies two videos of a Tesla crash on San Francisco's Bay Bridge: https://theintercept.com/2023/01/10/tesla-crash-footage-autopilot/. The Tesla changed lanes and braked abruptly, resulting in an eight-vehicle crash that injured nine people.

105. Preventative shutdowns of the self-driving Cruise are reported by Cade Metz, Photographs Jason Henry, "Stuck on the Streets of San Francisco in a Driverless Car," New York Times, October 14, 2022, https://www.nytimes.com/2022/09/28/technology/driverless-cars-san-francisco.html.

106. https://waymo.com/waymo-driver/ summarizes the features, but not the technology behind the features, of the Waymo Driver.

107. See Wikipedia "Function (mathematics)."

Chapter 14 Structure of Language

108. [Wittgenstein, 1963].

109. [Wittgenstein, 1958].

110. Preface [Wittgenstein, 1958].

111. For details about logical atomism and the picture theory, see Wikipedia "Tractatus Logico-Philosophicus," "Logical atomism," and "Picture theory of language." [Hülster, 2019] describes these concepts using numerous examples of the natural sciences.

112. The Tractatus establishes what we call here "conceptually consistent" via complex arguments involving the picture theory of the Tractatus. Intuitively speaking, all statements that make sense in some way are pictures of facts of the world.

113. A complete list of the statements covered by the *Tractatus* is as follows where we use the technical term "proposition" instead of "statement."

> *Meaningful Propositions*: convey information, may be
>   true or false
> *Pseudopropositions*: convey no information
>   *Meaningless Propositions*: are a priori true or false
>   *Tautologies*: are always true
>   *Contradictions*: are always false
>   *Nonsensical Propositions*: are neither true nor false

114. In 1930, Wittgenstein included in his notes a harsh critique of the ladder argument; see Wikipedia "Wittgenstein's ladder":
"I might say: if the place I want to get [to] could only be reached by way of a ladder, I would give up trying to get there. For the place I really have to get to is a place I must already be at now.
"Anything that I might reach by climbing a ladder does not interest me."

115. Later, Wittgenstein wrote that the *Tractatus* contained "grave mistakes" (German *schwere Irrtümer*) that could not be remedied. See Preface [Wittgenstein, 1958].

116. Rebecca Saxe tells how the neuroprocesses simulate what other people are thinking, in her presentation "How the Brain Invents the Mind," YouTube video `https://www.youtube.com/watch?v=Wn0PzB-iv5o`, delivered at the National Academy of Sciences colloquium "The Brain Produces Mind by Modeling," 2019.

Chapter 15 Machine Translation

117. [Pestov, 2021] summarizes the different phases of machine translation from the 1930s onward, with emphasis on the developments since 1950.

Chapter 16 Turing Test

118. See Wikipedia "Turing test."

119. We may also use Wittgenstein's idea of language games to demonstrate—but not prove—correctness of the assertion that the computer cannot match human performance.
To this end, we create statements by the observer followed by responses from the two boxes. For the computer, we imagine that we

rely on a web of facts, while for the human, we envision how a person might react. Two exchanges below show what we have in mind.

- Round 1:
  Observer: "Good morning, how are you?"
  Computer: "Fine, thank you."
  Human: "To tell the truth: My knee started acting up again last night, and this morning I had trouble getting here."

- Round 2:
  Observer: "Could you please tell me the shortest route to drive to the Roxy Theater?"
  Computer: "Sorry, the Roxy doesn't exist anymore. It was razed in 1985."
  Human: "Funny that you ask. Yesterday somebody had the same question. The Roxy was razed several decades ago for a supermarket. Why are you interested in the Roxy, if you don't mind my asking?"

Do you sense the model changes that take place in the observer and the human in the box? The computer just processes the information using the assumed web of facts.

You should have no trouble to extend the exchange. Each step demonstrates that the observer and human *interact* in a profound way, while the computer *reacts* using a web of facts.

Chapter 17 Chinese Room

120. See Wikipedia "Chinese room."

121. See Wikipedia "Artificial general intelligence" sections "History" and "Philosophical perspective." David Cole ranks the Chinese Room debate as follows: "[T]he Chinese Room argument has probably been the most widely discussed philosophical argument in cognitive science to appear in the past 25 years." https://plato.stanford.edu/archives/fall2004/entries/chinese-room/.

122. See Wikipedia "Chinese room" section "Replies."

Chapter 18 Artificial General Intelligence

123. See Wikipedia "Artificial general intelligence."

124. See Wikipedia "Holocene extinction."

Chapter 19 Classification Test

125. See Wikipedia "Computer chess."

126. For example, see Wikipedia "ChatGPT."

127. See Wikipedia "Computer music."

Chapter 20 Avoiding Blunders

128. See Wikipedia "Operations Research."

Epilogue

129. See Wikipedia "Leonhard Euler."

130. [Truemper, 2021].

131. [Truemper, 2022].

Bibliography

[Beck et al., 1979] Beck, A. T., Rush, A. J., Shaw, B. F., and Emery, G. (1979). *Cognitive Therapy of Depression*. Guilford Press.

[Bennett and Hacker, 2022] Bennett, M. R. and Hacker, P. M. S. (2022). *Philosophical Foundations of Neuroscience*. Wiley, Blackwell, second edition.

[Burns, 2008] Burns, D. D. (2008). *Feeling Good: The New Mood Therapy*. Harper.

[Burns, 2020] Burns, D. D. (2020). *Feeling Great: The Revolutionary New Treatment for Depression and Anxiety*. PESI Publishing & Media.

[Chabris and Simons, 2011] Chabris, C. and Simons, D. (2011). *The Invisible Gorilla: How Our Intuitions Deceive Us*. Broadway Paperbacks.

[Charniak and McDermott, 1985] Charniak, E. and McDermott, D. (1985). *Introduction to Artificial Intelligence*. Addison-Wesley.

[Conant and Ashby, 1970] Conant, R. C. and Ashby, W. R. (1970). Every good regulator of a system must be a model of that system. *International Journal of Systems Science*, vol. 1, pp. 89–97.

[Damasio, 2021] Damasio, A. (2021). *Feeling & Knowing*. Pantheon Books.

[Dastin, 2018] Dastin, J. (2018). Amazon scraps secret AI recruiting tool that showed bias against women. *Reuters*, 10 October 2018.

[Eagleman, 2020] Eagleman, D. (2020). *Livewired: The Inside Story of the Ever-Changing Brain*. Pantheon Books.

[Friston, 2010] Friston, K. (2010). The free-energy principle: A unified brain theory? *Nature Reviews Neuroscience*, vol. 11, pp. 127-138.

[Friston et al., 2021] Friston, K., Moran, R. J., Nagai, Y., Taniguchi, T., Gomi, H., and Tenenbaum, J. (2021). World model learning and inference. *Neural Networks*, December 2021, pp. 573-590.

[Ghorbani et al., 2019] Ghorbani, A., Abid, A., and Zou, J. (2019). Interpretation of neural networks is fragile. *Proceedings of the AAAI Conference on Artificial Intelligence*, vol. 33.

[Gibson et al., 2013] Gibson, A. S. C., De Koning, J. J., Thompson, K. G., Roberts, W. O., Micklewright, D., Raglin, J., and Foster, C. (2013). Crawling to the finish line: why do endurance runners collapse? Implications for understanding of mechanisms underlying pacing and fatigue. *Sports Medicine*, vol. 43, pp. 413–424.

[Grafton, 2020] Grafton, S. (2020). *Physical Intelligence: The Science of How the Body and the Mind Guide Each Other Through Life*. Penguin Random House.

[Hawking and Mlodinow, 2010] Hawking, S. and Mlodinow, L. (2010). *The Grand Design*. Bantam Books.

[Heaven, 2019] Heaven, D. (2019). Why deep-learning AIs are so easy to fool. *Nature*, 09 October 2019, https://www.nature.com/articles/d41586-019-03013-5.

[Hülster, 2019] Hülster, F. (2019). *Introduction to Wittgenstein's Tractatus Logico-Philosophicus*. Leibniz Company.

[Kabat-Zinn, 1990] Kabat-Zinn, J. (1990). *Full Catastrophe Living*. Dell Publishing.

[Kahneman, 2011] Kahneman, D. (2011). *Thinking, Fast and Slow*. Farrar, Straus, and Giroux.

[Kepler, 1627] Kepler, J. (1627). *Tabulae Rudolphinae (Rudolphine Tables)*. https://archive.org/details/tabulaerudolphin00kepl/page/n1/mode/2up. A book produced in 2014 contains the original Latin text and a German translation. It uses the fonts and graphics of the original book for both versions—an astonishing achievement. Title: *Die Rudolphinischen Tafeln*. Editor: Jürgen Reichert. Publisher: Königshausen & Neumann, 2014. See `https://www.amazon.de/Die-Rudolphinischen-Tafe ln-J%C3%BCrgen-Reichert/dp/3826053524`.

[Merritt, 1989] Merritt, D. (1989). *Building Expert Systems in Prolog*. Springer-Verlag.

[Mlodinow, 2022] Mlodinow, L. (2022). *Emotional: How Feelings Shape Our Thinking*. Pantheon Books.

[Mowbray et al., 2021] Mowbray, M., Savage, T., Wu, C., Song, Z., Cho, B. A., Rio-Chanona, E. A. D., and Zhang, D. (2021). Machine learning for biochemical engineering: A review. *Biochemical Engineering Journal*, vol. 172.

[Nestor, 2020] Nestor, J. (2020). *Breath: The New Science of a Lost Art*. Riverhead Books.

[Pestov, 2021] Pestov, I. (2021). A history of machine translation from the cold war to deep learning. *freeCodeCamp* #Machine Learning, 12 March 2018, `https: //www.freecodecamp.org/news/a-history-of-machine-trans lation-from-the-cold-war-to-deep-learning-f1d335ce8b5/`.

[Russell and Norvig, 2010] Russell, S. and Norvig, P. (2010). *Artificial Intelligence - A Modern Approach*. Third edition. Prentice Hall.

[Selinger et al., 2015] Selinger, J. C., O'Connor, S. M., Wong, J. D., and Donelan, J. M. (2015). Humans Can Continuously Optimize Energetic Cost during Walking. *Current Biology*, vol. 25, pp. 2452–2456.

[Straach and Truemper, 1999] Straach, J. and Truemper, K. (1999). Learning to ask relevant questions. *Artifical Intelligence*, vol. 111, pp. 301-327.

[Strickland, 2019] Strickland, E. (2019). How IBM Watson overpromised and underdelivered on AI health care. *IEEE Spectrum*, April 2019, `https://spectrum.ieee.org/how-ibm-watson -overpromised-and-underdelivered-on-ai-health-care`.

[Truemper, 2004] Truemper, K. (2004). *Design of Logic-based Intelligent Systems*. Wiley-Interscience.

[Truemper, 2021] Truemper, K. (2021). *Magic, Error, and Terror: How Models in Our Brain Succeed and Fail*. Leibniz Company.

[Truemper, 2022] Truemper, K. (2022). *Wittgenstein and Brain Science: Understanding the World*. Leibniz Company.

[Wielemaker et al., 2021] Wielemaker, J., Arias, J., and Gupta, G. (2021). s(CASP) for SWI-Prolog. *GDE'21:ICLP'21* (Virtual) Workshop on Goal-directed Execution of Answer Set Programs, https://ceur-ws.org/Vol-2970/gdeinvited4.pdf.

[Wittgenstein, 1958] Wittgenstein, L. (1958). *Philosophical Investigations*. Basil Blackwell; available at https://archive.org/detail s/philosophicalinvestigations_201911.

[Wittgenstein, 1963] Wittgenstein, L. (1963). *Tractatus Logico-Philosophicus*. Routledge & Kegan Paul Ltd; go to https://pe ople.umass.edu/klement/tlp/tlp.pdf for the German version and two translations into English.

[Zacks, 2020] Zacks, J. M. (2020). Event Perception and Memory. *Annual Review of Psychology*, vol. 71.

Acknowledgements

M. Grötschel and A. Rajan reviewed several versions and suggested improvements.

Technical advice or general help were provided by G. Gupta, P. M. S. Hacker, M. Kantarcioglu, and S. Truemper.

I. Truemper and U. Truemper were patient editors.

The University of Texas at Dallas—our home institution—made essential resources available.

We thank all of them for their help.

K. T.

Index